D1608714

IN SCHOOL WITH

JESUS

Connecting Teachers and Students in the Bible Each Day

3RD GRADE

Morning Bible Study

Cheryl Drozd

C STREET PUBLISHING

www.InSchoolWithJesus.com

3rd Grade Paperback ISBN: 978-1-952761-08-9
3rd Grade Kindle ISBN: 978-1-952761-09-6
Library of Congress Control Number: 2020909051
Cataloging in Publication Data on file with the publisher.

Scriptures are from the NIV Life Application Study Bible, ©2011 per copyright guidelines set forth by Tyndale House Publishers, Inc. and Zondervan.

Nihil Obstat, Reverend Michael Gutgsell, JCL, Censor Librorum,
Imprimatur Most Reverend George J. Lucas, Archbishop of Omaha, July 22, 2020, Omaha, NE

10 Commandments on www.InSchoolWithJesus.com
Nihil Obstat, Reverend Michael Gutgsell, JCL, Censor Librorum, July 22, 2020
Imprimatur Most Reverend George J. Lucas, Archbishop of Omaha, July 22, 2020, Omaha, NE

Publishing and Production: Concierge Publishing Services

Printed in the United States of America

10 9 8 7 6 5 4 3 2 1

Dedication

Dedicated to all the teachers who had the calling to teach in the
Catholic Schools. God brought you here for a reason.
Let's teach God's Word together.

CONTENTS

ZEPHANIAH

HAGGAI

ZECHARIAH

ACKNOWLEDGMENTS

Thank you, Lord, for being my light and standing with me through this all.

A special thank you to my family. My husband Joe, who has stood behind me with all my ventures in life. My daughter, Natalie, for her walk with me and the Lord in this beautiful experience together. My two boys, Cameron and Ben, who helped with the technology part and keeping Mom mentally healthy with their love. I am thankful for my blessing of family and all their talents.

Thank you to my parents for their love, prayers, and biggest fans I have in life.

I want to thank Father Joe for all his support and obvious belief in me. His encouragement is overwhelming.

Thank you to Father Swanton for all his love, support, and guidance. To Cheryl Zoucha who said to write this and all the staff, children, and parents at Saint Bonaventure, who piloted it and gave feedback.

A thank you to all my donors who made this curriculum possible.

The Omaha Dioceses and their part, and Carl and Jolene for their faith in me and the project. As my first donors, you allowed God to work in my heart to see this through.

Thank you to all my prayer warriors and Bible study groups who learned alongside me and supported my journey.

A special thank you to Rev. Matthew J. Gutowski for his suggestions, time, and perseverance to help get this study into a Catholic edition. Thank you to Rev. Michael Gutgsell also for his help on finishing the project.

Sending love to Pastor Mike, for his wonderful teachings of God's Word to me and to the Peter, James, and John in my life. You ladies are the backbone of how this all came into my world. I love you Kathy, Joyce, and Corenna.

NOTE FROM THE AUTHOR

Please take the time to read John 20:20-21, before beginning this study each year, and never let anything replace Jesus! He is the way of the truth, the path in life and He is sending you!

In Matthew 16:17-19, Jesus gives us the opportunity to bring people to the kingdom of heaven by showing them with the message of salvation found in God's Word. Only God is in control of His kingdom, but He uses us to help others find the way inside. To all who believe in Christ and obey His words, the kingdom doors are swinging wide open. Who will you gather this year to listen to His teachings and do your part on this journey they are taking through His book of lessons? What will God teach YOU this year?

I pray that you allow Jesus to work in you through his teachings and that you feel His presents alive in your classroom each day. Celebrate your God in prayer, music and time for knowledge as He gives you all the tools and strength that you need.

In Luke 11, Jesus teaches us how to pray and in verses 33-36, he teaches us about the Light Within. Let your light shine in your classroom and do not be afraid, as Jesus is with you and will walk this year by your side. Pray for his guidance and thank Him for all the blessings this year will bring. I can't even imagine teaching a classroom without his Word and not starting the day in prayer. You have been blessed to be where you are and you are exactly where you are supposed to be.

I thank you, Lord, for the love you have given me to want to help others. For the love I have for children and the special talents you gave me to connect with them. Thank you, Lord, for my desire to guide parents with the raising of their children and to help them let You be their light. I am so thankful for the love I have for teachers and the opportunity to work with them all through the blessings of You, God. Help me to be a good friend, love others above myself and to remember to always put You first in my day. Amen

God bless you on your journey.

Cheryl Drozd

HOW TO USE THIS CURRICULUM

It is always a good idea to read what is asked of you ahead of time. This gives God time to talk to you individually while you go over the reading, objectives, and discussion time. This is YOUR time with God. Let Him speak to you about how you can share your life with the kids through these lessons.

It is really important to answer the questions I ask you to share openly and honestly. Your students will connect with you on a deeper level once they see you as a "sinful human" just like them. We move closer to God when we share openly with others. It is a great testimony to share how God is still working in your life as an adult and that you don't have it all figured out either.

If you are unable to think of something that you can relate to the question asked, I give you some of my own examples to use. Take the time to share the author's experience as a story, so they can remember the lesson. It allows them to see how adults still make mistakes and learn from those mistakes. The closer you are to God, the easier it will be for you to share, as you will see.

Take time for discussion. If you are having trouble getting the class to open up, I provide answers to discussion questions to either get the ball rolling or for you to share and talk about if the class isn't there yet. The more you allow time for discussion, the easier it will be for them, so don't give up on it because it is an important part.

Under "materials," you will find things to look up and have on hand to enhance the lesson with a visual. Under "other resources," you might find some scripture to look up in other books of the Bible that will show consistency in God's Word or reinforce what is happening in what you are reading. Flip to those pages together or have them marked ahead of time.

A prayer is provided for you, but don't feel you have to use it. If you feel a prayer come in your heart, then speak the words to your class and pray it. I have found that certain lessons seem to go exactly with a situation happening in our classroom at the time, and we can work those into our prayer for the day. I allow God to teach me every year how to reach my students through these same lessons in different ways each time.

You will find that each year your class is different, so the discussion will go different ways as the students connect their lives with the lessons. Allow the Holy Spirit to work in your discussion and be okay with it going another direction if it does. You will also be in different seasons of life as you teach, so your examples and stories will change and have more meaning to you. I encourage you to share as you see God working in your life. Be empowered to acknowledge it.

If someone asks something you don't know the answer to, just simply say, "That will be a good question for us to look up and find the answer to for next class," or "Let's put that in our questions for Father and he can answer that for us." Don't feel you have to know everything, because you don't. You need to show them that you are human, right? We don't know all the answers, and we are not meant to. Learning our faith and drawing closer to God never ends. Just be real, follow through with what you say you will do, and learn together from it.

There are four lessons offered each week. Day five can be used many ways: a day of church, a day to either draw or journal about the week's lessons, do a Lectio Divina or WRAP on the first day, a day for prayer offering up praises and petitions, or another day to choose a different reading or what will be read in church on Sunday. You can read the day's verses or chapter word for word. Underline the parts you want to read to shorten it up some or read it ahead of time and tell it in your own words. Allowing the students to journal or draw while you read is also an option. If the same lines are read more than once in a week, you might have the class recap and tell what is happening for one of the days.

This curriculum can be done a few ways with how the Bible is read. The entire class can have a Bible to read from at the same time, but with this method, I would suggest everyone has the same Bible and have it be one they use through all their school years. I have suggestions for the Bibles I like best for an easy read on my website. Another suggestion is to allow the children to bring in their own Bibles and read from a different one each day, giving them some different wording to hear. With Pre-K, they would have different pictures to look at. I also give them a special day to take the Bible home and read it with their parents. You can choose the day you read their Bible in class as the evening they take it home or designate a certain night for family Bible night. Be creative with it but get them in it!

Be sure to download The 10 Commandments and the 10 Ways I Saw God Today from my website, so you can use them on a regular basis with your class. We want to live our lives through the Ten Commandments and open our eyes to seeing God's work in our lives daily.

TEACHERS!

1. We learn the Bible in our own way and through the ways God talks directly to us. We will all see things a little different and learn different things from different lessons, but that's the beauty of God's Word.

2. We aren't supposed to know it all. We learn through reading God's teachings in the Bible and listening when He talks to us individually. Then we go out and live the path He has set forth just for us.

You don't teach this Bible study; you take time, listen and change.

It's not about knowing everything. It's about taking time out for God, which becomes an example for others to reflect on His Word.

MORNING BIBLE STUDY

3RD GRADE - JONAH

There is no running from God!
Saying no to God quickly leads to disaster. Saying yes brings a
new understanding of God and His purpose in the world.

The book of Jonah is a story of a prophet's flight and how God turns him around. God shows Jonah that His message of salvation is for all people. Jonah doesn't agree with this, and so he runs in the opposite direction.

We will learn that it is better to obey God than to run away from Him. Our merciful God will give us another chance to serve Him when we return just as he did with Jonah. We can't run from God because He is in control. Instead, we need to allow Him to guide us in life.

JONAH WEEK 1

JONAH 1:1-3

Lesson 1

Takeaway: God told Jonah to go to Nineveh, where there was idolatry, unfaithfulness, witchcraft, evil plots against God, and unfair treatment of the helpless.

Takeaway: Jonah was supposed to preach to them and warn them of God's coming judgment. He was supposed to tell them they could receive mercy and forgiveness if they repented.

> **DISCUSSION:** HOW DO YOU THINK JONAH FELT ABOUT THIS TASK? GOD IS ALWAYS TEACHING US THROUGH OUR EXPERIENCES. WE HAVE TO DECIDE IF WE ARE GOING TO LEARN FROM THEM OR NOT.

Prayer: *Heavenly Father, we thank you for the lessons you teach us each day. Open our hearts and eyes so we may learn from the opportunities you provide for us. Help us make the right choices to follow your path for us. We want to learn from you, our all-knowing and Almighty God. Amen.*

Lesson 2

Takeaway: Jonah didn't want the people of Nineveh to receive God's mercy. He grew up not liking them.

Takeaway: Not wanting to share God's love with others was a sinful attitude.

MATERIALS

The Bible

The story of Noah. This can be another story to refer to about how crazy God's task sounded.

NOTES

NOTE TO TEACHERS
DISCUSSION: WHEN YOU SEE ITEMS IN ALL CAPS, THEY ARE NOTES TO SHARE WITH YOUR CLASS. (Notes in parentheses are notes and thoughts for the teacher.)

. . . .

DISCUSSION: DO YOU EVER WISH UNHAPPINESS ON SOMEONE? (Example: Maybe hoping they won't make the team or will mess up their dance solo so everyone will see their mistake and not think they are the best dancer in class.) WHEN WE ACCEPT GOD'S LOVE, WE MUST ALSO LEARN TO ACCEPT ALL THOSE WHOM HE LOVES. WE WILL FIND IT MUCH EASIER TO LOVE OTHERS WHEN WE TRULY LOVE GOD.

Prayer: *God, we know your love is everlasting and that you forgive and love all. Help us be better about loving those around us, especially those who are different from us. Put love in our hearts, so we are open to getting to know them better and seeing their gifts from you. May we be images of your Son Jesus here on earth, loving everyone and helping them find a relationship with you as well. Amen.*

Lesson 3

Takeaway: God had a special mission for Jonah, but he didn't want to do it.

Takeaway: Jonah went the opposite way God told him to go.

DISCUSSION: GOD NEVER GIVES YOU MORE THAN YOU CAN HANDLE. HE WILL BE THERE WITH YOU THROUGH EVERYTHING. ANY TIME YOU HAVE SOMETHING HARD IN YOUR LIFE, KNOW THAT IT'S GOD'S WAY OF TRAINING AND PREPARING YOU FOR HIS PLAN FOR YOUR LIFE. YOU CAN'T RUN FROM GOD.

Prayer: *Lord, we ask that you give us direction by working on our hearts while in prayer, quiet time, and through signs throughout our day. Help us obey your plan for us and feel the strength of your love beside us as we face things in life that are scary or difficult. We know you are always with us. Amen.*

. . . .

Lesson 4

Takeaway: God loves other people, including those not of our group, background, race, or denomination.

Takeaway: God wants His people to proclaim His love in words and actions to the whole world.

> **DISCUSSION:** GOD WANTS US TO BE HIS MISSIONARIES WHEREVER WE ARE AND WHEREVER HE SENDS US. (Club soccer team, prayer at the dinner table at home, or calling out a friend when they do something wrong.)

Prayer: *Help us, God, do our best to spread the Good News of your love to others and never be ashamed of our faith and relationship with you. We ask that you place your shield of armor on us and give us the strength we need to be your disciples. Amen.*

JONAH WEEK 2

JONAH 1:4-9

Lesson 1

Takeaway: Jonah was endangering the lives of the ship's crew because he disobeyed God.

Takeaway: Jonah was being **selfish**.

- *Selfish:* lacking consideration for others and concerned mainly with one's own personal profit or pleasure.

  DISCUSSION: WE HAVE A RESPONSIBILITY TO OBEY GOD'S WORD BECAUSE OUR SIN AND DISOBEDIENCE CAN HURT THOSE AROUND US. DOES ANYONE HAVE A GOOD EXAMPLE OF THAT OR HOW THAT COULD HAPPEN? (Example: You steal the recess whistle from the teacher so that when you go out for recess, she can't blow the whistle for you to come in. The teacher says no one is allowed to go out to recess until the whistle is returned, and all your classmates suffer for it.)

Prayer: *Lord Jesus, we know that we can all be selfish at times and that it is hard to always do the right thing. Please remind us to turn to you for support and direction in what we should do in our lives. Help us put others first as you did, Jesus. You are a perfect example for us. Amen.*

MATERIALS
The Bible

NOTES

NOTE TO TEACHERS
DISCUSSION: WHEN YOU SEE ITEMS IN ALL CAPS, THEY ARE NOTES TO SHARE WITH YOUR CLASS. (Notes in parentheses are notes and thoughts for the teacher.)

- -

Lesson 2

Takeaway: Jonah was sound asleep below the deck while the storm raged on.

Takeaway: Jonah's actions didn't seem to bother his conscience.

> **DISCUSSION:** WE CANNOT MEASURE OBEDIENCE BY THE WAY WE FEEL, BUT RATHER COMPARE WHAT WE DO TO GOD'S STANDARDS FOR LIVING. JUST BECAUSE YOU ARE OK WITH IT, DOESN'T MEAN GOD IS OK WITH IT. YOU CAN NOT RUN FROM GOD. (Example: Your parents asked you to clean your room on Saturday, but instead, you choose to play video games in your room all day, breaking commandment number four. Are you putting your games above obeying your parents as God asks of you and being ok with that? We must follow commandment number four.)

Prayer: *Heavenly Father, we know your commandments, and we want to live by them. Help us listen more clearly to the messages you send our hearts. We know we can look to you for guidance and direction. We want to do the right thing even when it's easier to choose the wrong thing. We don't want to disobey you. Amen.*

Lesson 3

Takeaway: The crew cast lots so they could find the guilty person.

Takeaway: They relied on their superstitions for the answer, and it only worked because God intervened to let Jonah know that he couldn't run away from Him.

> **DISCUSSION:** SUPERSTITIONS ARE NOT GOD LED. WE MUST TURN TO THE LORD FOR CLARITY.

Prayer: *Lord, we need to remember to pray and ask for your guidance when it comes to making decisions in our lives. Help us allow time for learning what you want us to know. We need prayer, time to reflect, and an open heart to hear your message and find peace in the decisions we make. Amen.*

Lesson 4

Takeaway: You can't want God's love and run away from Him at the same time.

Takeaway: You can't say you truly believe in God if you don't follow what He teaches you.

> **DISCUSSION:** ARE YOU SHOWING YOUR MOM LOVE WHEN YOU DISOBEY HER AND CAUSE HER TROUBLE? WE SHOW LOVE WITH KINDNESS, TRUST, AND FORGIVENESS. BE CONSCIOUS OF YOUR ACTIONS TOWARDS OTHERS.

Prayer: *Lord God, we know the only way to truly show our love for you is to follow you and show others how to do the same. Help us do this by putting you first in all that we do and respecting our parents, our teachers, and other adult leaders in our lives. May we also be kind and loving to our siblings and classmates even when it is difficult. We know that with your help, we can show love and feel your love in our hearts. Amen.*

JONAH WEEK 3

JONAH 1:10-16

Lesson 1

Takeaway: Jonah knew the storm was his fault because he disobeyed God, but he didn't say anything until he lost the toss when the crew cast lots.

Takeaway: Jonah refused to go to Nineveh, but he was willing to give his life to save the sailors.

> **DISCUSSION:** JONAH'S HATRED FOR NINEVEH WAS MESSING UP HIS THINKING. OUR EYES GET CLOUDED AND CAN'T SEE WHAT WE ARE DOING WHEN WE HAVE HATRED IN OUR HEARTS.
>
> **DISCUSSION:** TAKE A LOOK INTO YOUR HEART AND START PRAYING FOR GOD'S HELP TO REMOVE ANY HATRED AND FIND FORGIVENESS SO YOUR EYES CAN SEE CLEARLY AND YOUR HEART IS CLEAN.

Prayer: *Lord, we have a hard time loving everyone and know that this is what you ask us to do. Help us open our hearts to those who are hard to love and see the good that they have to offer. Help us see that we are all your children and can learn from one another. Amen.*

Lesson 2

Takeaway: The sailors showed more compassion than Jonah by trying to save his life.

MATERIALS
The Bible

NOTES

NOTE TO TEACHERS
DISCUSSION: WHEN YOU SEE ITEMS IN ALL CAPS, THEY ARE NOTES TO SHARE WITH YOUR CLASS. (Notes in parentheses are notes and thoughts for the teacher.)

Takeaway: Jonah had no compassion for the Ninevites and did not want to warn them of God's coming judgment.

> **DISCUSSION:** GOD WANTS US TO BE CONCERNED FOR ALL OF HIS PEOPLE.

Prayer: *Lord, we pray for all of your people. Help those who have not yet found you in their lives turn to you and start feeling your love and work in their lives. We ask you to forgive those who choose other things above you, as they do not know the true meaning of life here on earth. Amen.*

Lesson 3

Takeaway: Jonah had disobeyed God by running away, but he stopped and **submitted** to God.

- ◆ *Submit* – to accept or yield to a superior force or the authority or will of another person. God teaches us to submit to Him and to our leaders.

Takeaway: When the storm stopped, the crew began to pray to God and vowed to serve Him.

> **DISCUSSION:** GOD USES OUR MISTAKES TO HELP OTHERS KNOW HIM. ADMITTING OUR SINS CAN BE A POWERFUL EXAMPLE TO OTHERS. WHEN WE START DOING SOMETHING TO STOP OUR SIN AND WORK HARD NOT TO DO IT AGAIN, THAT BRINGS US CLOSER TO GOD. THIS IS ALSO HOW YOU EARN TRUST AGAIN WITH YOUR PARENTS OR TEACHERS. GOD LOOKS FOR THE SAME ACTIONS AND CHANGE IN YOUR HEART.

Prayer: *Heavenly Father, we give you our hearts. We ask for your forgiveness for the mistakes we make. May we find ways to change*

. . . .

and go another direction that will make you proud. Help us be humble, allow others to see us fail, and draw closer to you because of it. Amen.

Lesson 4

Takeaway: The Bible says pride is destructive and separates us from God.

Takeaway: God wants us to be humble. We should turn to Him and trust in our faith to feel peace when we go through the storms of life.

> **DISCUSSION:** TO PURSUE HUMILITY, WE NEED TO BEGIN EACH DAY ACKNOWLEDGING OUR DEPENDENCE ON GOD, GIVING HIM ALL THE GLORY AT THE END OF THE DAY, LOOKING FOR GOOD IN OTHERS, AND ENCOURAGING AND HELPING OTHERS EVERY DAY.

Prayer: *Lord, may we keep our eyes on the cross and begin each day by acknowledging your presence in our lives. May we give the glory to you each day and give grace to others. Help us, Lord, encourage and serve others in your name. Amen.*

JONAH WEEK 4

JONAH 1:17 – JONAH 2

Lesson 1

Takeaway: Christ used Jonah's experience as an illustration of His death and resurrection. (Matthew 12:39-41)

Takeaway: Jesus was making it clear to the religious leaders of the day that they would be judged for their stubbornness and disbelief.

> **DISCUSSION:** WHILE THE PEOPLE OF NINEVEH WILL RESPOND TO JONAH SPEAKING GOD'S WORD, THE RELIGIOUS LEADERS DURING THE TIME OF JESUS REFUSED TO BELIEVE GOD'S WORD SPOKEN BY HIS VERY OWN SON. WE HAVE BOTH THE STORY OF JONAH AND THE DEATH AND RESURRECTION OF CHRIST AS SIGNS OF GOD'S WORK. WHAT ARE OTHER WAYS WE SEE SIGNS OF GOD'S WORK? (How He gives us the right words to say when we ask, in our blessings each day, and through the love we receive from others.)

Prayer: *Lord God, we see your work in our everyday lives and know that you work in us through our feelings about what to do and how to handle things. You give us small signs of blessings and eye-opening experiences to keep us on track and know that you are here. May we continue to see you and trust in your guidance. Amen.*

MATERIALS

The Bible

The 10 Ways I Saw God Today can be found on the website for Lesson 3.

OTHER RESOURCES

Matthew 12:39-41 for Lesson 1.

NOTE TO TEACHERS
DISCUSSION: WHEN YOU SEE ITEMS IN ALL CAPS, THEY ARE NOTES TO SHARE WITH YOUR CLASS. (Notes in parentheses are notes and thoughts for the teacher.)

· ·

Lesson 2

Takeaway: Jonah gives a prayer of thanksgiving for not drowning rather than praying for deliverance.

Takeaway: God heard his prayer from inside the fish.

> **DISCUSSION:** YOU CAN PRAY ANYWHERE AND AT ANY TIME, AND GOD WILL HEAR YOU. NOTHING IS TOO DIFFICULT FOR GOD.

Prayer: *Lord Jesus, we thank you so much for answering our prayers. Sometimes the answers are not exactly what we want, but with time and guidance, we can learn the reason behind them. You always know what is best for us, Lord, and in this, we trust and believe. Amen.*

Lesson 3

Takeaway: When life is going well, we may forget about God and take Him for granted, but when we are scared or overwhelmed, we hear ourselves cry out to Him.

Takeaway: When we have a consistent, daily commitment to God, we develop a solid relationship with Him.

> **DISCUSSION:** LOOK TO GOD DURING BOTH THE GOOD AND BAD TIMES, AND YOU WILL HAVE A STRONGER SPIRITUAL LIFE. (This is why we focus on the ten ways God works in our lives each day. There are more than ten ways, but when we start looking, we start seeing, and we can begin rejoicing with praise. God is here with us through it all, and we need to strengthen our relationship with Him, by looking and talking to Him daily.)

Prayer: *Lord, we praise you for all that you do and all the beauty in the world. Help us see and recognize you in our lives. May we find our ten ways to glorify you daily. Amen.*

Lesson 4

Takeaway: It took a miracle to get Jonah to do as God had commanded.

Takeaway: Jonah's story began with a tragedy, but things would have gotten worse if God had allowed him to keep running.

> **DISCUSSION:** WHEN YOU KNOW GOD WANTS YOU TO DO SOMETHING, DON'T RUN. GOD MAY NOT STOP YOU AS HE DID JONAH. (Give an example of when you felt God asked you to do something. For me, it was to write this Bible curriculum. I felt the need to help classrooms and families find a simple way to put God's Word first each day. God laid it on my heart and continued to direct me through the whole process. I had to be patient and obedient.)

Prayer: *Heavenly Lord, we want to walk on the path you have given us. If we get off that path, we ask you to please guide us back and face whatever we need to. We know that you will be there with us through it all and draw us closer to you, Lord. We are here to do your will. Amen.*

JONAH WEEK 5

JONAH 3

Lesson 1

Takeaway: Jonah preached God's message of doom to one of the most powerful cities in the world.

Takeaway: When we bring God's Word to others, we shouldn't let the pressures of fear or acceptance dictate our words.

> **DISCUSSION:** WE ARE CALLED TO SHARE GOD'S MESSAGE AND HIS TRUTH, NO MATTER HOW UNPOPULAR IT MAY BE. HOW IMPORTANT IS IT FOR YOU TO FOLLOW THE CROWD? ARE YOU OK WITH BEING DIFFERENT, STANDING OUT, AND STANDING UP FOR GOD? WHEN WAS A TIME YOU WERE CHALLENGED WITH THIS OR MIGHT BE IN THE FUTURE? (Laughing at someone behind their back, choosing to hold that drink in your hands and take a sip when others are watching, being rude to your mom in front of your friends.)

Prayer: *Lord, we pray for you to be with us during these challenging times in our lives. When we feel insecure or weak because of peer pressure, rest the strength of your love on our shoulders and help us stand up and do your work. Amen.*

Lesson 2

Takeaway: The Word of God is for everyone.

Takeaway: The people of Nineveh were open to God's message and immediately repented from their wickedness.

MATERIALS
The Bible

OTHER RESOURCES
Jeremiah 18:7-8 for Lesson 4.

NOTE TO TEACHERS
DISCUSSION: WHEN YOU SEE ITEMS IN ALL CAPS, THEY ARE NOTES TO SHARE WITH YOUR CLASS. (Notes in parentheses are notes and thoughts for the teacher.)

• •

> **DISCUSSION:** JUST BECAUSE SOMEONE IS NOT RAISED IN A CHRISTIAN HOME, DOESN'T MEAN THEY DON'T HAVE THE DESIRE TO HAVE A RELATIONSHIP WITH CHRIST. LET OTHERS KNOW OF YOUR RELATIONSHIP WITH HIM AND HOW HE WORKS IN YOUR LIFE DAILY. INVITE THEM TO BE OPEN TO HIM WORKING IN THEIR LIFE AND SUGGEST THEY LOOK FOR TEN WAYS THEY SEE HIM DAILY ALSO, OR EVEN START WITH FIVE. BE A DISCIPLE OF CHRIST. PRAY FOR STRENGTH WITH THIS.

Prayer: *Lord God, we want to spread your Word to everyone and be the disciples you need us to be. Give us the strength to speak up, words to encourage others, and a heart that feels your love and guidance through it all. Amen.*

Lesson 3

Takeaway: God's words had an amazing effect on the people of Nineveh as they listened to Jonah's message and repented.

Takeaway: God's chosen people, the Israelites, had heard many messages from the prophets, but they had refused to repent, yet the Ninevite people only needed to hear God's message once.

> **DISCUSSION:** IT IS NOT JUST ABOUT HEARING GOD'S WORD THAT PLEASES HIM, BUT HOW WE OBEDIENTLY RESPOND TO IT. WHAT DO YOU THINK THAT MEANS? (It isn't about reading the Bible; it's about how you respond to the Bible and live your life.)

Prayer: *God, we pray that we work hard to make good choices today and be good followers of Christ. May we not only listen to your Word but also live it in our lives daily, spreading your love to others and showing them the joy of following you. Amen.*

Lesson 4

Takeaway: God responded to the people with mercy and canceled His threatened destruction.

Takeaway: God said in Jeremiah 18:7-8 that He would save any nation on which He had pronounced judgment if it repented.

> **DISCUSSION:** THE PURPOSE OF GOD'S JUDGMENT IS TO HELP US CORRECT OUR SINS. GOD FORGAVE BOTH JONAH AND NINEVEH FOR TURNING THEIR WRONGS INTO RIGHTS. HOW CAN WE DO THIS IN OUR LIVES? (Always think of Jesus when making choices in life, pray for God's help with sins that are hard to stop doing.)

Prayer: *Heavenly Father, we pray to be more like Jesus in everything we face today. Help us show compassion to others and seek your guidance when we are unsure or scared. We want to always look for ways we can turn any sin around and change for your glory. Amen.*

JONAH WEEK 6

JONAH 4

Lesson 1

Takeaway: Jonah might have been a little more concerned about his own reputation than God's.

Takeaway: He knew that if the people repented, none of his warnings to Nineveh would come true. While this might embarrass him, it would give glory to God.

> **DISCUSSION:** ARE YOU MORE INTERESTED IN GIVING GLORY TO GOD OR YOURSELF? ALL THAT YOU DO AND THE TALENTS THAT YOU HAVE ARE GOD-GIVEN. GIVE THANKS FOR ALL YOUR BLESSINGS AS GOD IS GOOD AND ALL-DESERVING!

Prayer: *Heavenly Father, we want to praise and thank you for all that we have, all that we are, and all that you do! May we always remember to give you the glory for everything good that happens and be thankful for any trials you put us through, as we know that you are growing us through those times. Amen.*

Lesson 2

Takeaway: Jonah was concerned about the shriveled plant, but not over what could have happened to Nineveh.

Takeaway: Most of us have been sad over the loss of a pet or something important to us that has broken, but have you ever been sad for a person who doesn't know God?

MATERIALS
The Bible

The song "I Can Only Imagine" by MercyMe for Lesson 3.

NOTES

NOTE TO TEACHERS
DISCUSSION: WHEN YOU SEE ITEMS IN ALL CAPS, THEY ARE NOTES TO SHARE WITH YOUR CLASS. (Notes in parentheses are notes and thoughts for the teacher.)

• •

> **DISCUSSION:** LET'S PRACTICE BEING MORE SENSITIVE TO THE SPIRITUAL NEEDS OF PEOPLE AROUND US INSTEAD OF OUR OWN INTERESTS. TODAY WE WILL PRAY FOR THOSE WHO DON'T KNOW GOD AND CONTINUE TO PRAY THROUGHOUT THE DAY FOR THEM. (Set a timer every hour or four times a day to stop and pray for those who don't have a relationship with God.)

Prayer: *Lord, we pray for those who don't know you. We ask you to lay your hands upon them and touch their hearts. May you guide them and let them feel your presence. Amen.*

Lesson 3

Takeaway: Most people want to tear down those who are wicked and have done wrong by punishing them.

Takeaway: God is merciful and feels compassion for the sinners we want judged. He has plans to bring them to Himself.

> **DISCUSSION:** WHAT IS YOUR ATTITUDE TOWARD OTHERS WHO SEEM WICKED? DO YOU WANT THEM PUNISHED OR TO EXPERIENCE GOD'S MERCY AND FORGIVENESS? HAVE YOU EVER BEEN FORGIVEN BY SOMEONE? HOW DOES IT FEEL? (Parents forgive all the time. Imagine if they didn't forgive you, what would life be like then?)
>
> **DISCUSSION:** PLAY THE SONG "I CAN ONLY IMAGINE" BY MERCYME. PRAY IN SONG TODAY. THINK ABOUT WHAT IT WILL FEEL LIKE TO SEE JESUS IN HEAVEN SOMEDAY. PRAY FOR OTHERS TO HAVE THIS EXPERIENCE TOO AND FOR GOD TO WORK IN THEIR HEARTS. FEEL THE SONG, CLOSE YOUR EYES, AND IMAGINE.

Prayer if song is not possible: *Lord, we are so thankful for your forgiveness, love, and loyalty to us. We are so excited about Heaven and to someday meet you. Help us forgive others and prepare our hearts for the joyful time of living with you eternally. Amen.*

Lesson 4

Takeaway: God spared the sailors when they pleaded for mercy, Jonah when he prayed from inside the fish, and the people of Nineveh when they responded to Jonah's preaching.

Takeaway: God answers the prayers of those who turn to Him.

> **DISCUSSION:** GOD WILL ALWAYS WORK HIS WILL. HE DESIRES THAT EVERYONE COMES TO HIM, TRUSTS IN HIM, AND HAS A RELATIONSHIP WITH HIM. WHEN WE TURN TO GOD AND ARE OBEDIENT, WE WILL RECEIVE HIS MERCY AND NOT HIS PUNISHMENT. PRACTICE BUILDING YOUR RELATIONSHIP WITH GOD DAILY. (Through prayer, quiet time, reading the Bible, changing things in your life that are sinful, or just checking in with Him throughout the day.)

Prayer: *God, we praise you today for your mercy! Help us listen and follow your commands throughout our lives. When it is difficult, may we turn to you and your Word for answers and guidance. You are so worthy of our praise. Amen.*

MORNING BIBLE STUDY

3RD GRADE - MICAH

There is no running from God!

Saying no to God quickly leads to disaster.
Saying yes brings a new understanding of God and
His purpose in the world.

Micah shows us a true picture of God, who hates sin and loves the sinner. We will see God's judgment on Israel, Judah, and the whole earth. We will see God's anger in action when He judges and punishes sin, but we will also see God's love in action as He offers eternal life to all who repent and believe.

Micah will show us what it means to be a faithful person of God and live according to His will.

MICAH WEEK 7

MICAH 1:1-7

Lesson 1

Takeaway: God will bring judgment on the false prophets, dishonest leaders, and selfish priests in Israel and Judah.

Takeaway: They were privately wanting to gain money and power while publicly carrying out religious ceremonies.

> **DISCUSSION:** YOU CANNOT MIX SELFISH MOTIVES WITH LIVING A LIFE FOR GOD. WE NEED TO BE AWARE OF OUR TENDENCY TO BE SELFISH. REMEMBER TO ALWAYS PUT GOD AND OTHERS BEFORE YOURSELF.

Prayer: *Heavenly Father, we ask for guidance and a heart for others. May we see the good in everyone and choose to be kind and loving toward them. Help us put their needs above our own and not let our selfishness get in the way of friendships and family. Amen.*

Lesson 2

Takeaway: Choosing to live your life apart from God is simply making a commitment to sin.

Takeaway: Sin leads us to an emptiness in our hearts and God's judgment..

MATERIALS
The Bible

A picture or a list of the twelve tribes of Israel for Lesson 3.

NOTES

NOTE TO TEACHERS
DISCUSSION: WHEN YOU SEE ITEMS IN ALL CAPS, THEY ARE NOTES TO SHARE WITH YOUR CLASS. (Notes in parentheses are notes and thoughts for the teacher.)

. . . .

> **DISCUSSION:** ONLY GOD CAN SHOW US THE WAY TO ETERNAL PEACE. HE DISCIPLINES US TO KEEP US ON THE RIGHT PATH. WHAT DO YOU THINK ETERNAL PEACE MEANS? (Heaven, the feeling inside to always want to do good and no longer want to hurt others.) HOW DOES GOD DISCIPLINE US? (Through our trials and hard times in life, He keeps reminding us that we are nothing without Him. We can't take things on ourselves; we need to always turn to Him.)

Prayer: *Lord, we love the thought of eternal peace. Having that feeling inside that we can feel at ease and have no worries or hurt, sounds amazing. We thank you for your discipline, just as we thank you for our parents and the other adults in our lives who help us through their teachings. May we respect them and you through it all. Amen.*

Lesson 3

Takeaway: There were twelve tribes of Israel under David and Solomon. After Solomon's death, the kingdom divided into two parts. (Provide a picture or a list of the twelve tribes.)

Takeaway: Judah and Benjamin stayed loyal to David's line under Solomon's son, who ruled as their king. They made up the southern kingdom called Judah with Jerusalem as their capital city. The other ten tribes became the northern kingdom, also called Israel, with Samaria as their capital city.

> **DISCUSSION:** THE DESTRUCTION OF SAMARIA IS FULFILLED JUST AS MICAH PREDICTED. GOD SENT HIS SON JESUS AS OUR MESSENGER. WHAT MESSAGE DID HE DELIVER TO US? (That we should love others the way we want to be loved and turn away from our sins by turning to Him instead.)

• •

Prayer: *Lord God, we pray for love in our hearts and to stop the hate we feel at times. May we always feel your love as we work through the pain we feel. Guide us to choose prayer instead of hatefulness. Amen.*

Lesson 4

Takeaway: Micah's message identifies two sins: the way they chose to worship and their unfairness to others.

Takeaway: Within the capital cities, these sins entered and infected the entire country.

> **DISCUSSION:** MICAH MAKES IT CLEAR THAT GOD HATES THESE THINGS AND STILL DOES TODAY. BUT GOD IS VERY WILLING TO PARDON THE SINS OF ANY WHO REPENT. WHAT DOES IT MEAN TO REPENT? (To truly be sorry and ask for forgiveness and then turn the other way, no longer allowing that sin in your life again, going to confession in your church.) USE THIS TIME TO REPENT OF ANYTHING YOU FEEL YOU NEED TO TODAY.

Prayer: *Father, we ask you to put upon our hearts any sin that you feel we need to deal with today. Help us clean our hearts and start over. We want to repent and move away from this sin. Thank you for your mercy and love. Amen.*

MICAH WEEK 8

MICAH 1:8-16

Lesson 1

Takeaway: Samaria's sins had become incurable and would soon be fatal. God's judgment on the city was already beginning.

Takeaway: Samaria's sin had also influenced Jerusalem, and judgment would come to them as well.

> **DISCUSSION:** HAVE YOU NOTICED HOW WHEN SOMEONE STARTS SOMETHING, THERE IS ALWAYS ANOTHER THAT WILL FOLLOW AND THIS FOLLOWING CONTINUES TO SPREAD THROUGHOUT THE SCHOOL, COMMUNITY, OR COUNTRY? WHEN WE ARE INFLUENCED BY PEOPLE WHO PUT THINGS ABOVE GOD OR ARE UNKIND TO OTHERS, WE ARE COMMITTING THE SAME KINDS OF SINS AS SAMARIA. THESE HISTORY STORIES ARE HERE FOR US TO LEARN FROM. WHAT CAN WE DO TODAY TO BETTER OURSELVES IN THESE TWO AREAS? (Take time out for God each day and be kind to everyone in class; not be part of the following but choose a different path others can follow.)

Prayer: *Lord God, help us be kind to everyone, and not just to those who are easy to have friendships with. May we reach out to all people and show friendship and love to all as we praise you daily for the gifts and talents you have given us. Help us to not just follow others but rather to make our own choices in the directions we choose to go with you leading us the whole way. Amen.*

MATERIALS
The Bible

NOTES

NOTE TO TEACHERS
DISCUSSION: WHEN YOU SEE ITEMS IN ALL CAPS, THEY ARE NOTES TO SHARE WITH YOUR CLASS. (Notes in parentheses are notes and thoughts for the teacher.)

. . . .

Lesson 2

Takeaway: Micah preached about God's judgment to city after city, emphasizing the need for justice and peace because of the people's sins.

Takeaway: Micah plays the role of a lawyer for God's case against Israel, Judah, their leaders, and their people.

> **DISCUSSION:** TRUE FAITH IN GOD GENERATES KINDNESS, COMPASSION, JUSTICE, AND HUMILITY. WE CAN PLEASE GOD BY SEEKING THESE ATTRIBUTES IN OUR SCHOOL, FAMILIES, CHURCH, AND NEIGHBORHOODS. WHAT DO THESE ATTRIBUTES LOOK LIKE? (Being nice to others and caring about them, standing up for those who are being treated wrongly and giving all glory to God.)

Prayer: *God, we want to show kindness and compassion in our work here at school, during the time spent with family, when at church, and out in our community. May we do things with a happy heart and find joy in doing right by you. Amen.*

Lesson 3

Takeaway: The people of Lachish had swayed many to follow their evil example.

Takeaway: When we sin, others tend to follow our example.

> **DISCUSSION:** YOU MAY NOT CONSIDER YOURSELF A LEADER, BUT OTHERS OBSERVE YOUR ACTIONS AND WORDS AND MAY CHOOSE TO FOLLOW YOUR EXAMPLE WITHOUT YOU EVEN KNOWING IT. OUR GOAL IN LIFE IS TO ALWAYS PORTRAY THE LIGHT OF JESUS IN OUR HEARTS.

Prayer: *Heavenly Father, please come into our hearts and let others see you in us. May we be good examples for others on how to love, respect, and honor you through our actions, words, and thoughts. Let your Son be our example to follow. Amen.*

Lesson 4

Takeaway: Micah warns the people in verse fifteen how the land surrounding Adullam had numerous caves that the leaders of Judah would be forced to go and hide in when the enemy approached.

Takeaway: Micah also shared the sorrow the parents would feel as their children were taken to a distant land to be slaves.

> **DISCUSSION:** TAKE SOME TIME TO THINK ABOUT WHAT THIS MUST HAVE FELT LIKE FOR THESE PEOPLE. THEY HAD TO GO INTO HIDING AND WERE SEPARATED FROM THEIR PARENTS AND MADE SLAVES. WE ARE SO FORTUNATE TO HAVE OUR FAMILY TOGETHER AND LIVE IN A SAFE HOME.

Prayer: *Lord God, we thank you for our families. Thank you for our homes, our safety, and the love we feel for those we care about. May we never take our families for granted and show love and kindness daily in our homes. Amen.*

MICAH WEEK 9

MICAH 2

Lesson 1 (Micah 2:1-2)

Takeaway: Micah stands up against those who make plans to do evil deeds at night and then get up at dawn to do them.

Takeaway: A person's thoughts and plans reflect their character.

> **DISCUSSION:** WHAT DO YOU THINK ABOUT AS YOU LAY DOWN TO SLEEP? WHAT ARE TEN WAYS YOU SAW GOD IN YOUR LIFE? SOME THINGS YOU ARE GOING TO TRY AND DO BETTER TOMORROW? ARE YOU PRAYING FOR OTHERS AND THANKING GOD FOR ALL YOU HAVE? HOW DO YOU END EACH DAY?

Prayer: *Heavenly Father, remind us to end each day with you in our hearts and minds. Help us take the time to be thankful for the things you give us and pray for those in need, rather than focusing on our own needs. Amen.*

Lesson 2 (Micah 2:3-7)

Takeaway: God was not taking revenge on Israel for rejecting what was true. He wanted them to get back on the right path.

Takeaway: They needed a firm discipline like a child to keep them going in the right direction.

MATERIALS
The Bible

NOTES

NOTE TO TEACHERS
DISCUSSION: WHEN YOU SEE ITEMS IN ALL CAPS, THEY ARE NOTES TO SHARE WITH YOUR CLASS. (Notes in parentheses are notes and thoughts for the teacher.)

DISCUSSION: IF WE ONLY WANT TO HEAR GOD'S COMFORTING MESSAGES, WE MAY MISS OUT ON WHAT HE HAS TO TEACH US. LISTEN WHEN GOD SPEAKS TO YOUR HEART, EVEN WHEN THE MESSAGE IS HARD TO TAKE. (Share a time when it was hard for you to listen to what God was asking of your heart. For me, I had a good friend of mine tell me she was going to take charge of our Bible study group because I had too much on my plate and wasn't organized enough to be in charge. It hurt to have her say that. I didn't want to give up my role, but I also knew that it was God telling me that I needed to let some things go and do a better job with the time that I set aside for Him.) GOD WILL SPEAK TO YOU THROUGH OTHERS AND IN YOUR HEART. YOU JUST NEED TO BE READY TO LISTEN. TALK ABOUT HOW DISCIPLINE IS HELPFUL AND WHY IT'S IMPORTANT TO STAY ON THE RIGHT TRACK.

Prayer: *Lord, we thank you for the discipline in our lives. Help us stay on the path you have set forth for us. When we do wrong, help us understand why it isn't right and give us the people in our lives who care enough to teach us your ways. May we be good students and disciples. Amen.*

Lesson 3 (Micah 2:8-11)

Takeaway: The people liked the false prophets because they told them only what they wanted to hear.

Takeaway: Micah spoke out against the prophets who encouraged people to feel comfortable in their sin.

DISCUSSION: A TRUE TEACHER OF GOD SPEAKS THE TRUTH, EVEN WHEN THE PEOPLE DON'T WANT TO HEAR. WHEN YOU DON'T AGREE WITH WHAT AN ADULT IS TELLING YOU, YOU NEED TO THINK ABOUT "WHAT WOULD JESUS DO?" WHEN WE CHOOSE TO DO THINGS AGAINST WHAT JESUS WOULD DO, WE ARE MOST LIKELY SINNING. CHECK YOUR HEART, REVIEW THE TEN COMMANDMENTS, AND FACE YOUR SIN BY MAKING A CHANGE.

• •

Prayer: *Lord, help us respect the commandments that you gave us. When we feel unsure about something we did or are being asked to do, give us the strength to check our hearts, remind us to review your Word to make the right choice, and help us be strong in our decision. Amen.*

Lesson 4 (Micah 2:12-13)

Takeaway: Micah shares two future events here. Judah will return from captivity in Babylon, and all the believers will gather when the Messiah returns.

Takeaway: God gave His prophets the ability to have visions of various future events, but not necessarily the ability to say when these events would happen. The purpose was not to predict exactly how things would occur but that they would.

> **DISCUSSION:** THESE PREDICTIONS HELPED THE PEOPLE TURN AWAY FROM SIN BY GIVING THEM HOPE. WHAT KIND OF HOPE HAS GOD GIVEN US? (That we will go to Heaven someday and be united with Him.) WE MUST TURN TO GOD DAILY AND OFFER OUR LIVES TO HIM. ALLOW HIM TO USE YOU HOWEVER HE SEES FIT DURING YOUR TIME HERE ON EARTH, KNOWING THAT ONE DAY YOU WILL LIVE WITH HIM IN HIS KINGDOM IN HEAVEN AND HAVE ETERNAL LIFE.

Prayer: *Heavenly Father, we are so blessed to have you as our God. We look forward to meeting you someday. Help us do what you need us to while we are here on earth and help our hearts follow you as we wait for the promise you have given of eternal life in Heaven. Amen.*

MICAH WEEK 10

MICAH 3

Lesson 1 (Micah 3:1-7)

Takeaway: Micah publicly declared the sins of the leaders, who were priests, prophets, and those responsible for teaching the people right from wrong.

Takeaway: The leaders, who knew the law and should have taught it to the people, had become the worst sinners, taking advantage of the people they were supposed to serve.

> **DISCUSSION:** ALL SIN IS BAD, BUT THE SIN THAT LEADS OTHERS AWAY FROM GOD IS THE WORST OF ALL. THE TEN COMMANDMENTS TELL US HOW TO LIVE OUR LIVES. GOD IS OUR BEST EXAMPLE OF ALL THAT IS GOOD. CHRISTIANS SHOULD POINT OTHERS IN THE DIRECTION OF GOD'S WISDOM BY LIVING THEIR LIVES ACCORDING TO HIS PURPOSES. ALWAYS LOOK FOR GOD IN OTHERS AND THOSE YOU CHOOSE TO LEARN FROM.

Prayer: *Lord God, we want to lead others to you, not push them away. Let your Son be our daily example of how to love and show your love to everyone around us. May we practice the Ten Commandments every day. Amen.*

Lesson 2 (Micah 3:1-7)

Takeaway: The difference between right and wrong can sometimes be blurred, but spiritual leaders are supposed to help others understand it.

MATERIALS
The Bible

OTHER RESOURCES
Acts 1:8 and Ephesians 1:11 for Lesson 4.

NOTE TO TEACHERS
DISCUSSION: WHEN YOU SEE ITEMS IN ALL CAPS, THEY ARE NOTES TO SHARE WITH YOUR CLASS. (Notes in parentheses are notes and thoughts for the teacher.)

. . . .

Takeaway: The Bible is God's guidebook showing us how to tell between right and wrong.

> **DISCUSSION:** WHO DO YOU LEAD IN YOUR LIFE? WHAT KIND OF EXAMPLE ARE YOU FOR THEM? (Siblings, younger kids in school. Showing them how to walk down the halls, how to pray, and how to see the good in others.)

Prayer: *Lord, we ask for your guidance when we lead others to follow you. We aren't always aware of those who look up to us and want direction or leadership. Help us work hard at being a good example and leader to those who follow in our footsteps. Amen.*

Lesson 3 (Micah 3:1-7)

Takeaway: The leaders didn't have a heart for those they were supposed to serve.

Takeaway: They treated the people terribly to satisfy their own desires, and then asked for God's help when they found themselves in trouble.

> **DISCUSSION:** WE SHOULDN'T TREAT GOD LIKE A LIGHT SWITCH TO BE TURNED ON ONLY AS NEEDED. WE SHOULD ALWAYS RELY ON HIM. MAKE GOD A PART OF EVERY DAY, EVERY DECISION, AND BEFORE WE START ANYTHING. WE MUST ALWAYS REMEMBER TO PRAY. WHEN ARE SOME OTHER TIMES WE CAN ADD PRAYER INTO OUR DAY HERE AT SCHOOL? (Before tests, before recess, before a fieldtrip, or before church asking for His presence in our hearts and minds.)

Prayer: *Heavenly Father, help us turn to prayer throughout our days. Not only when we need something, but also when we want to reflect, be thankful, or just ask for direction. May we always turn to you for guidance and praise. Amen.*

Lesson 4 (Micah 3:8-12)

Takeaway: The power of the Holy Spirit worked through Micah's ministry. The Holy Spirit also empowers us.

Takeaway: Jesus told His followers they would receive power to witness about Him when the Holy Spirit came on them. (Acts 1:8)

DISCUSSION: YOU CAN'T SEE GOD'S WORK BY RELYING ON YOUR OWN STRENGTH. ONLY WHEN WE RELY ON THE POWER OF THE HOLY SPIRIT, CAN WE TRULY WITNESS HIM THROUGH OUR LIVES.

DISCUSSION: GOD WORKS IN ALL THINGS ACCORDING TO HIS WILL. (Ephesians 1:11) GOD'S WILL IS THE ULTIMATE REASON FOR EVERYTHING THAT HAPPENS. WE ARE HERE TO LEARN AND TURN TO HIM WITH EVERYTHING WE DO.

Prayer: *We ask for your strength, Lord, in times of need, when we feel weak and just need your guidance. Help us do things according to your plan for us. We are here to serve you and turn to the path you have planned for us. Amen.*

MICAH WEEK 11

MICAH 4

Lesson 1 (Micah 4:1-8)

Takeaway: The phrase in verse one, "in the latter days," describes the time when God will reign over His perfect kingdom. This will be a time of peace and a blessing of the end to all war forever.

Takeaway: The phrase "mountain of the Lord" refers to Mount Zion.

> **DISCUSSION:** WE DO NOT KNOW HIS DATE, BUT GOD HAS PROMISED THAT HE WILL COME AGAIN. (See also Isaiah 2:2, Jeremiah 16:15, Joel 3:1.)

Prayer: *Lord, we look forward to the latter days. May you bring peace and blessings on all of the earth. Help us work toward a world without war until your kingdom comes. Amen.*

Lesson 2 (Micah 4:9-13)

Takeaway: Micah predicted the Babylonian captivity, even before Babylon became a powerful empire.

Takeaway: God promises us a time of peace and prosperity, but He also promises His judgment and punishment for all who refuse to follow Him.

> **DISCUSSION:** WE CAN BE CERTAIN ABOUT BOTH PROMISES.

MATERIALS
The Bible

OTHER RESOURCES

Isaiah 2:2, Jeremiah 16:15, and Joel 3:1 for Lesson 1.

2 Chronicles 36:9-23 for Lesson 3.

NOTE TO TEACHERS
DISCUSSION: WHEN YOU SEE ITEMS IN ALL CAPS, THEY ARE NOTES TO SHARE WITH YOUR CLASS. (Notes in parentheses are notes and thoughts for the teacher.)

Prayer: *We know you are true to your promises, Lord. Help us live as you intended and be confident of the coming Judgment Day. We want you to know that we are your faithful followers. Amen.*

Lesson 3 (Micah 4:9-13)

Takeaway: Micah predicted a drastic statement to the people of Judah when he told them that there would be an end of the kings. They thought their kingdom would last forever.

Takeaway: Micah also said that Babylon would carry away the king of Judah after they destroyed the land, and God would later help His people return to their land.

> **DISCUSSION:** THIS ALL HAPPENED JUST AS MICAH SAID IT WOULD, AND YOU CAN FIND THESE EVENTS RECORDED IN 2 CHRONICLES 36:9-23. GOD KEEPS HIS PROMISES.

Prayer: *Heavenly Father, we give you our promise that we will follow your commandments the best that we can. When we fail, we ask for you to pick us up and help us keep trying to do better. You are our strength and hope. Amen.*

• •

Lesson 4

Takeaway: When God reveals the future, it is for His purpose. He isn't doing it to satisfy our curiosity.

Takeaway: He wants us to know about the future so that we can change our present behavior.

> **DISCUSSION:** FOREVER BEGINS NOW, AND KNOWING HE FULFILLS HIS PROMISES SHOULD MOTIVATE FOR US TO SERVE HIM, NO MATTER WHAT THE REST OF THE WORLD MAY BE DOING.

Prayer: *Lord God, help us follow you and shut out the rest of the world who don't see who you are right now. We pray for them and all people that they may know, love, and honor you as we should. Amen.*

MICAH WEEK 12

MICAH 5

Lesson 1 (Micah 5:1-5)

Takeaway: The last of the kings in David's line was Zedekiah.

Takeaway: Micah said that the next king would be the Messiah, who would establish a kingdom that would never end.

> **DISCUSSION:** THE OLD TESTAMENT TELLS US THAT JESUS WILL COME, AND HE DOES. GOD FOLLOWS THROUGH WITH HIS PROMISES.

Prayer: *Lord, we thank you for your Son and the example He is for us in our lives. May we grow to be good examples of this as well. Amen.*

Lesson 2 (Micah 5:1-5)

Takeaway: Jerusalem's leaders were proud of all their wealth and power, but Micah preached that even with all its wealth and power, Jerusalem would not be saved.

Takeaway: Bethlehem, a tiny town, would be the birthplace of the Messiah. He would be born as a baby and eventually would reign as the eternal King.

> **DISCUSSION:** PEOPLE WAITED FOR JESUS FOR MANY, MANY YEARS. HE SAYS HE WILL RETURN. WE NEED TO BE READY FOR THAT DAY.

MATERIALS

The Bible

NOTES

NOTE TO TEACHERS
DISCUSSION: WHEN YOU SEE ITEMS IN ALL CAPS, THEY ARE NOTES TO SHARE WITH YOUR CLASS. (Notes in parentheses are notes and thoughts for the teacher.)

· ·

Prayer: *God, we want to prepare for the return of your Son Jesus Christ. Help us grow closer to Him as we learn more about Him and His example for us. May we be humbly ready for His return by working at this daily. Amen.*

Lesson 3 (Micah 5:1-5)

Takeaway: Micah's words of seven shepherds and eight princely men is his way of saying that the Messiah will raise up many good leaders when He returns to reign.

Takeaway: "The Assyrians" in verse five refers to all nations in every age of time that opposed God's people.

> **DISCUSSION:** THESE GOOD LEADERS WILL BE THE ONES TO HELP CHRIST DEFEAT ALL EVIL IN THE WORLD.

Prayer: *Heavenly Father, we pray for all of our leaders. May we be good leaders too as we turn to you daily with decisions and choose to follow the path that you have set forth for us. Amen.*

Lesson 4 (Micah 5:6-15)

Takeaway: When God rules in His eternal kingdom, His strength and deliverance will not be found in military power but in His almighty power.

Takeaway: God will destroy all weapons, and armies will not be needed because God will be in the heart of every person.

> **DISCUSSION:** INSTEAD OF FEARING AN INVASION OF SOME KIND OR A NUCLEAR ATTACK, WE SHOULD HAVE CONFIDENCE IN GOD.

Prayer: *Lord, we trust in your power and know that you are in control of everything. We are confident, knowing that you have our best interests in mind as you continue to teach and grow us all here on earth. We know you are in control, not us. Amen.*

MICAH WEEK 13

MICAH 6

Lesson 1 (Micah 6:1-8)

Takeaway: God called to the mountains to serve as His witnesses to confirm the guilt of the people where they had built altars and sacrificed to false gods.

Takeaway: God reminds the people of all the ways they have been wrong towards Him and others.

> **DISCUSSION:** ANYTIME WE DO WRONG TO OTHERS, WE ARE ALSO DOING WRONG TO GOD. WHAT COMMANDMENTS MIGHT WE BREAK WHEN WE HURT OTHERS? (Two, four, five, six, seven, eight, nine, and ten.)
>
> **DISCUSSION:** GOD WANTS US TO LOVE OTHERS!

Prayer: *Lord, we ask you to put any false gods that we have in our lives on our hearts today. May we honor and love you first above anything else that may be getting in our way. We only want to glorify you, Lord. Amen.*

Lesson 2 (Micah 6:5)

Takeaway: Acacia Grove was the Israelite campsite where they received many of the instructions about how God wanted them to live.

Takeaway: Gilgal was the Israelite campsite where the people renewed their covenant with God.

MATERIALS

The Bible

See the way I teach the 10 Commandments on my website for Lesson 1.

Use The 10 Ways I Saw God Today off the website for Lesson 2.

Lesson 3 has some things to list somewhere to refer to during prayer times.

OTHER RESOURCES

1 Kings 16:21-26 and 29-33 for Lesson 4.

NOTE TO TEACHERS
DISCUSSION: WHEN YOU SEE ITEMS IN ALL CAPS, THEY ARE NOTES TO SHARE WITH YOUR CLASS. (Notes in parentheses are notes and thoughts for the teacher.)

. . . .

> **DISCUSSION:** THESE PLACES REPRESENT HOW GOD LOVES AND CARES FOR HIS PEOPLE. WHEN WE FORGET HOW FORTUNATE WE ARE AND TAKE GOD'S GIFTS FOR GRANTED, WE BECOME SELF-CENTERED.
>
> **DISCUSSION:** REMEMBER GOD'S GOODNESS DAILY AND THANK HIM. (Help them use The 10 Ways I Saw God Today on a regular basis.)

Prayer: *Heavenly Father, we want to thank you for all we have and all that you do for us. We know that we are so undeserving as we continue to sin, yet you forgive us and allow us to continue to make it right with you. Thank you for that. Amen.*

Lesson 3 (Micah 6:6-8)

Takeaway: Israel wanted God to leave them alone, so they tried to satisfy Him with sacrifices.

Takeaway: God only wants to transform our hearts through His love.

> **DISCUSSION:** ARE YOU FAIR WITH OTHERS? DO YOU SHOW MERCY TO THOSE WHO HAVE SINNED AGAINST YOU? ARE YOU PRACTICING HUMILITY? (List these somewhere to refer to during pray times.) EXAMINE THESE AREAS ON A REGULAR BASIS AS YOU WORK TO PLEASE GOD.

Prayer: *God, we want to be fair to others and love them as we would want them to love us back. Help us forgive others and open our hearts to ask for forgiveness when we have wronged someone. Let us humble ourselves, Lord, putting you above everything else and only giving you the glory for all our happiness and joy. Amen.*

Lesson 4 (Micah 6:9-16)

Takeaway: Omri led the people into idol worship when he reigned over Israel. His son, Ahab, was the most wicked king Israel ever had. (1 Kings 16:21-26, 29-33)

Takeaway: The people were in bad shape for following the commands and practices of these kings.

• •

DISCUSSION: TODAY, LET'S PRAY FOR THE LEADERS IN OUR COUNTRY THAT THEY MAY TURN TO GOD FOR GUIDANCE DAILY AND DO WHAT IS BEST IN HIS EYES WHEN MAKING DECISIONS.

Prayer: *Lord God, we pray for all the leaders in our country, community, and school. May they find direction in you for all the decisions and trials that they face. We pray that they will seek and follow your guidance daily. Amen.*

MICAH WEEK 14

MICAH 7:1-7

Lesson 1

This chapter begins with gloom and ends in hope.

Takeaway: Micah watched as the people decayed around him. Rulers commanded gifts, judges participated in bribes, and corruption was everywhere.

Takeaway: But God promised He would lead the people out of this darkness of sin and into His light.

> **DISCUSSION:** GOD ALONE IS PERFECTLY FAITHFUL. LET'S PRAISE GOD FOR WHO HE IS AND HIS FAITHFULNESS TO US.

Prayer: *Lord, we thank you for who you are. We know that you are so faithful to us and want to take time to praise you for that and appreciate all that you are. May we honor you in our day today. Amen.*

Lesson 2 (Micah 7:1-4)

Takeaway: Micah was unable to find an honest person anywhere in the land.

Takeaway: Even today, believers sometimes compromise Christian principles so they can do what they want. (Example: "It's ok if the grocery store gave me too much change back. I shop here often, so I deserve it.")

MATERIALS
The Bible

NOTES

NOTE TO TEACHERS
DISCUSSION: WHEN YOU SEE ITEMS IN ALL CAPS, THEY ARE NOTES TO SHARE WITH YOUR CLASS. (Notes in parentheses are notes and thoughts for the teacher.)

> **DISCUSSION:** WE CANNOT RATIONALIZE SIN. THE STANDARDS COME FROM GOD, NOT SOCIETY. WE ARE TO BE HONEST WITH GOD BECAUSE GOD IS TRUTH, AND WE ARE TO BE LIKE HIM.

Prayer: *God, we pray for guidance to keep us on our Christian path in life. Help us grow daily and open our eyes and hearts to your teachings. Amen.*

Lesson 3 (Micah 7:5-6)

Takeaway: Sin had affected government leaders, families, and the core of society in general.

Takeaway: Only God's judgment could purify the people. He needed to restore them from the inside out.

> **DISCUSSION:** WHAT ARE WAYS GOD USES HIS POWER TO DRAW THE NATION BACK TO HIM? (Hurricanes, tornadoes, times when people come together and are thankful for what they still have and for those who come to help them.) LET'S PRAY FOR OUR NATION TO COME TOGETHER AND STAY TOGETHER UNDER GOD'S GUIDANCE AND LOVE.

Prayer: *Heavenly Father, we pray for our nation. We ask for your people to come together under your guidance and love. May we find a way to break through these worldly ways of living and put you first as a nation. Amen.*

Lesson 4 (Micah 7:7)

Takeaway: Micah showed great faith in God and waited upon Him both personally and on Israel's behalf. He proclaims that he would wait upon God because God hears and saves when help is needed. God would bring His people through tough times.

• •

Takeaway: Israel must be patient in their punishment because God would bring them out of the darkness and punish their enemies.

> **DISCUSSION:** WE, TOO, CAN HAVE A RELATIONSHIP WITH GOD EVEN THROUGH TOUGH TIMES. ALL IT TAKES IS FAITH IN GOD AND A WILLINGNESS TO ACT ON THAT FAITH.

Prayer: *God, we pray for faith in our community and our world. May we see you in our daily lives and feel your presence with us through all things. Nothing is too big or too small for your power. Amen.*

MICAH WEEK 15

MICAH 7:8-20

Lesson 1 (Micah 7:8-13)

Takeaway: Micah understood that God would forgive His people if they remained patient and obedient.

Takeaway: God punished the people to bring them back to Him.

> **DISCUSSION:** DON'T BE ANGRY WITH GOD WHEN YOU ARE RECEIVING A PUNISHMENT FOR A SIN. INSTEAD, TURN AWAY FROM YOUR SIN AND TURN TO GOD.

Prayer: *Help us, Lord, be patient when we receive punishment for our sins. Allow us to learn from our mistakes and be more obedient the next time we are faced with the temptation. May we turn to you, Lord, and find strength in going the opposite direction from sin. Amen.*

Lesson 2 (Micah 7:14-20)

Takeaway: God is full of mercy.

Takeaway: He forgives and does not hold grudges when we repent.

> **DISCUSSION:** GOD OFFERS FORGIVENESS TO ALL WHO CONFESS THEIR SINS. CONFESS TODAY AND RECEIVE HIS LOVING FORGIVENESS.

MATERIALS

The Bible

NOTES

NOTE TO TEACHERS
DISCUSSION: WHEN YOU SEE ITEMS IN ALL CAPS, THEY ARE NOTES TO SHARE WITH YOUR CLASS. (Notes in parentheses are notes and thoughts for the teacher.)

. . . .

Prayer: *God, we offer up our hearts today and ask you to lay upon them any sins we need to acknowledge so we can repent and change the direction we have been going. (Allow some time for silence.) Help us, Lord, find a way to resist the temptation of our sins and turn to you for guidance and love through the struggle. Amen.*

Lesson 3 (Micah 7:14-20)

Takeaway: Micah said what God expected of His people, and it still holds true today.

Takeaway: We must do what is right, have mercy on others, and walk humbly with God.

> **DISCUSSION:** ONLY WHEN WE LIVE ACCORDING TO GOD'S WAY WILL WE MAKE A DIFFERENCE IN OUR HOMES, SCHOOL, AND COMMUNITY.

Prayer: *Lord, we want to grow in our faith with you and make a difference in our homes, school, and community. May others learn by our examples and see our faith through our actions and love for others. Make us disciples of yours, Lord. Amen.*

Lesson 4

Takeaway: Micah showed faith in God by:

1. Waiting on His timing.
2. Trusting He would bring them through the tough times.
3. Helping the Israelites accept God's punishment.
4. Knowing that their enemies would be punished in God's time.

> **DISCUSSION:** WAIT, TRUST, ACCEPT, AND BELIEVE. HOW DO THESE WORDS BRING US CLOSER IN OUR FAITH? (We must wait on God's timing, trust in His work, accept what He puts in front of us, and always believe in Him.)

Prayer: *Heavenly Father, we ask you to give us patience in our lives and help us trust in your ways. May we accept the things you put in our path to grow us and believe in your plan for us. Amen.*

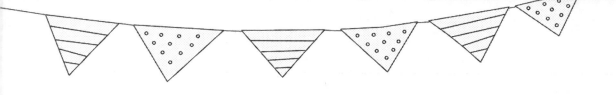

MORNING BIBLE STUDY

3RD GRADE - NAHUM

There is no running from God!

Saying no to God quickly leads to disaster. Saying yes brings a new understanding of God and His purpose in the world.

In the book of Nahum, God pronounces His judgment on Assyria for their disobedience, lack of interest in Him, and their rebellion against His control.

The prophet shows us that no ruler or nation gets away with rejecting Him. God settles all accounts. We can be sure that God's power and justice will conquer all evil.

Learn to trust in God and choose to live under His commands, rules, and guidelines for life.

NAHUM WEEK 16

NAHUM 1:1-5

Lesson 1

Takeaway: No one can hide from God's judgment.

Takeaway: If we trust in God, He will keep us safe.

> **DISCUSSION:** GOD RULES ALL OF HISTORY, THE WORLD, AND OUR LIVES. ONLY GOD CAN CHANGE THINGS, NOT HUMANS. HE WORKS THROUGH US. THROUGH THE GOOD AND HARD TIMES, HE IS AT WORK.

Prayer: *Heavenly Father, we know your power, and we always need your protection. Help us find you in everything that we do and through all situations, good or bad. May we allow you to work through us, doing what you need each day. Amen.*

Lesson 2

Takeaway: Nahum was a prophet for Nineveh, like Jonah.

Takeaway: Although Jonah had seen Nineveh repent a century earlier, the city had fallen back into evil ways. Nahum proclaimed God's anger about it.

> **DISCUSSION:** WE, TOO, CAN FALL BACK INTO SINS THAT WE HAVE TRIED TO TURN AWAY FROM. WE MUST TRUST IN GOD AND ASK FOR HIS FORGIVENESS. WHAT ARE SOME THINGS YOU CAN DO TO KEEP YOU FROM REPEATING A PAST SIN? (Leave your phone in your room during dinner, so it won't cause you to disrespect your family time. Have something nice ready to say about the person your friends always talk bad about at lunch so you can say that instead.)

MATERIALS
The Bible

OTHER RESOURCES

Deuteronomy 4:24 and 5:9 and see the way I teach the Ten Commandments on my website for Lesson 3.

NOTE TO TEACHERS
DISCUSSION: WHEN YOU SEE ITEMS IN ALL CAPS, THEY ARE NOTES TO SHARE WITH YOUR CLASS. (Notes in parentheses are notes and thoughts for the teacher.)

• •

Prayer: *God, we know that your power and justice will one day conquer all the evil in this world. Help us do our part here on earth by finding ways to stay away from sin and be the disciples you need us to be. Amen.*

Lesson 3

Takeaway: God's "jealousy" is His justice, which draws us to His purpose and His holiness. This is not retribution but discipline in a right attitude and action and blessing in mercy. (Deuteronomy 4:24 and 5:9)

Takeaway: When humans are jealous, they are most likely acting selfishly.

> **DISCUSSION:** WHAT COMMANDMENT IS ABOUT ENVY? (Number ten.) WHEN WE ARE ENVIOUS OF OTHERS, IT IS USUALLY ABOUT SOMETHING WE WANT TO CHANGE IN OUR OWN LIVES OR SOMETHING WE NEED TO WORK AT MORE. WE GET JEALOUS WHEN OTHERS HAVE WHAT WE WANT FOR OURSELVES. (Give an example of something you were envious of that you look back on and understand what the feelings were really about. For me, I was once really envious of a classmate who was a really good cheerleader from another town who came to our school. I was jealous of all the new cheers she brought to the squad and how much everyone liked her. Looking back, I see I should have focused more on how her talents helped improve our squad instead of being envious and disliking her for the person God made her to be. I should have worked on bringing the squad together instead of pulling them apart and taking sides.)

Prayer: *Lord, help us not be jealous of others. Work through our lives to heal old wounds or disappointments that have left us envious of others. May we turn to you, Lord, for answers and directions in our situations and better ourselves through your love. Amen.*

. . . .

Lesson 4

Takeaway: Some people don't believe in God because there is so much evil in the world.

Takeaway: God is slow to anger and gives His followers time to share His love and truth with those who choose evil.

> **DISCUSSION:** GOD WILL NOT ALLOW SIN TO GO ON FOREVER. BE THANKFUL THAT GOD GIVES PEOPLE TIME TO TURN TO HIM. WE MUST PRAY FOR THOSE WHO NEED TO TURN TO GOD FOR HELP AND FORGIVENESS IN THEIR LIVES.

Prayer: *God, we pray for all those who have not been blessed with the joy of knowing who you are. Rest next to them, Lord, and help them see your love and graciousness. May we help others see you through our hearts and be whatever you need us to be for them. Amen.*

NAHUM WEEK 17

NAHUM 1:6-15

Lesson 1 (Nahum 1:6)

Takeaway: God holds all things in balance and in tension.

Takeaway: Nothing on earth is more powerful than our awesome God.

> **DISCUSSION:** WE CAN FIND COMFORT IN KNOWING GOD WILL BE HERE FOREVER. WHAT WE MIGHT SEE AS A MOUNTAIN OF A PROBLEM, HE SEES AS A SPECK OF DUST. LEAVE ALL YOUR WORRIES BEHIND AND TRUST IN GOD.

Prayer: *Lord God, we pray that we can trust in you more. Help us grow in our faith by not worrying about the small things and just trusting in your plan. May we have peace in our hearts through our faith in you. Amen.*

Lesson 2 (Nahum 1:6-8)

Takeaway: For people who don't believe in God, His punishment feels like an angry fire.

Takeaway: For those who love Him, they see His mercy as a stronghold that will continue to supply them with all their needs.

> **DISCUSSION:** GOD GIVES US FREEWILL TO DECIDE WHAT KIND OF RELATIONSHIP WE WANT WITH HIM. WHAT IS SOMETHING YOU CAN DO TODAY TO CONTINUE TO GROW YOUR RELATIONSHIP WITH HIM? (Talk to Him more, spend more time asking Him to help with your decision-making, thank Him more throughout your day.)

MATERIALS

The Bible

NOTES

NOTE TO TEACHERS
DISCUSSION: WHEN YOU SEE ITEMS IN ALL CAPS, THEY ARE NOTES TO SHARE WITH YOUR CLASS. (Notes in parentheses are notes and thoughts for the teacher.)

Prayer: *Lord, we want to continue to grow in our relationship with you each day even though it takes work. Remind us of your presence each morning and throughout our day. May we take the time to praise you and enjoy all that you give us as we continue to build our trust and faith in you. Amen.*

Lesson 3 (Nahum 1:9-11)

Takeaway: Nineveh resisted obeying God.

Takeaway: They would be destroyed for rebelling against Him.

> **DISCUSSION:** WHAT ARE SOME THINGS WE REBEL AGAINST? (Going to church, praying before bed or meals, honoring our parents, or using God's name in vain.) LET'S REPENT IN SILENCE AND MAKE A CHANGE BY CHOOSING TO GO THE OTHER WAY.

Prayer: *Lord, we think that we are doing everything right, but there is always something we can work on. No one is perfect, except you. As humans, we still have a lot of work to do. Help us be faithful to the work and honor our commitment to you by following your lead in life. Amen.*

Lesson 4 (Nahum 1:12-15)

Takeaway: The good news for Judah was that God would destroy all of their wickedness.

Takeaway: Whether you like it or not or believe in Him or not, God always wins and will forever reign.

> **DISCUSSION:** WE CAN'T CONTROL THE OUTCOME OF THINGS IN LIFE, BUT GOD CAN. WE MUST ALWAYS TURN TO HIM AND TRUST HIM WITH ALL THINGS. START EACH MORNING IN THE PRESENCE OF GOD, END EACH EVENING REFLECTING ON HIS WORK IN YOUR LIFE, AND GROW IN YOUR TRUST AND FAITH.

Prayer: *Lord God, we trust you to grow us into the disciples you need us to be. May we continue to learn through our study in your Word and reflect on the areas in our lives we can improve on. We put all our trust in you. Amen.*

NAHUM WEEK 18

NAHUM 2

Lesson 1 (Nahum 2:1-5)

Takeaway: Two separate kingdoms had formed following Solomon's reign and a dispute that had happened with his son.

Takeaway: Ten of the tribes became the northern kingdom, and Judah and Benjamin remained together as the southern kingdom, staying loyal to David's line.

> **DISCUSSION:** WHAT ARE THINGS THAT SEPARATE OUR WORLD INTO "KINGDOMS?" (Politics, religions, race, neighborhoods, schools, states, countries.) HOW CAN WE COME TOGETHER? (Pray, listen to one another, be more open and trust God to lead, be happy for others and not so stubborn.)

Prayer: *Lord God, we pray for unity in our homes, school, community, and world. Help us listen to one another and take time to pray on things. May we turn to you for the right answers and unify under you and your plan. We pray for all nations under God. Amen.*

Lesson 2 (Nahum 2:6-7)

Takeaway: Verse six could refer to either the enemy flowing into Nineveh like a flood or possibly an actual flood from an enormous amount of water flowing out of the opened dam gates into Nineveh.

Takeaway: Verse seven is a reference to Nineveh's queen.

MATERIALS

The Bible

Display a list of the twelve tribes of Israel.

Stop, Pray, and Turn the Other Way off the website for Lesson 4.

NOTES

NOTE TO TEACHERS
DISCUSSION: WHEN YOU SEE ITEMS IN ALL CAPS, THEY ARE NOTES TO SHARE WITH YOUR CLASS. (Notes in parentheses are notes and thoughts for the teacher.)

• •

> **DISCUSSION:** NINEVEH IS AN EXAMPLE TO ALL THAT NO ONE IS INVINCIBLE. GOD'S POWER AND JUSTICE WILL ONE DAY CONQUER ALL EVIL, AND WE CAN BE CONFIDENT IN THAT. NEVER UNDERESTIMATE THE POWER OF GOD!

Prayer: *Lord, we know how powerful you are, and it helps us feel safe, knowing you always have a plan and will guard us. Help us pray through times of destruction and disasters, knowing that you are in charge. We can find comfort in your power and control. Amen.*

Lesson 3 (Nahum 2:8-3:1)

Takeaway: The people of Nineveh were wealthy because they took it from other nations.

Takeaway: They had taken money from innocent people to maintain their luxurious standard of living, depriving others so they could live excessively.

> **DISCUSSION:** DEPRIVING INNOCENT PEOPLE IS A SIN THAT ANGERS GOD. HOW CAN WE BE BETTER ABOUT THIS IN OUR LIVES AS CHRISTIANS? (Give when we can, donate instead of throwing things away, use our talents to help in other countries.)

Prayer: *Heavenly Father, we pray for those who are less fortunate than us. Help us find ways to use our resources and talents for others. May we pray for them and care about their well-being rather than being selfish and prideful. Amen.*

Lesson 4

Takeaway: God had given the people of Nineveh a chance to repent, and they did after hearing Jonah but then returned to their sinful lives.

Takeaway: There is a point when a person has gone too far, and there is no turning back. Assyria was at this point.

> **DISCUSSION:** WE CAN'T KEEP SAYING WE ARE SORRY AND CONTINUE TO SIN THE SAME SIN OVER AND OVER. WE MUST GIVE IT ALL TO GOD AND TURN TO HIM FOR DIRECTION AND STRENGTH. (Use Stop, Pray, and Turn the Other Way from the website.)
>
> **DISCUSSION:** HOW CAN WE HELP OTHERS WITH THIS? (When someone is living in sin, we can ask them to turn to God, pray for them, and let them know we are praying for them, but it is up to them to repent and change.)

• •

Prayer: *God, we know that we must repent after sinning, turn the other direction, and no longer allow that sin into our lives. Remind us it is never too late to repent and start again. May we work hard, honor you, and be conscious of your ways every day. Amen.*

NAHUM WEEK 19

NAHUM 3

Lesson 1 (Nahum 3:1-7)

Takeaway: Nineveh made false friendships with other nations.

Takeaway: Then, when the other nations relaxed, thinking they were friends, Nineveh destroyed them.

> **DISCUSSION:** NINEVEH WAS IMPRESSIVE ON THE OUTSIDE AND DECEITFUL ON THE INSIDE. DON'T ALLOW ANYONE TO LOWER YOUR STANDARDS OR COMPROMISE YOUR MORAL PRINCIPLES SUCH AS THE TEN COMMANDMENTS. LET'S REVIEW THEM AND SEE WHY WE WOULDN'T WANT TO BE A PART OF ANYTHING THAT DIDN'T AGREE WITH ALL OF THEM.

Prayer: *Lord, we pray for your guidance when choosing activities, groups, and peers. Open our eyes and ears to find ones that properly match our values so that we can encourage one another under your leadership. Amen.*

Lesson 2 (Nahum 3:8-13)

Takeaway: Judah was surrounded by Nineveh, and the situation seemed hopeless.

Takeaway: Thebes (No Amon) was a city in Egypt that Nineveh had conquered fifty-one years before. God said that the same violence done in Thebes would happen in Nineveh.

MATERIALS

The Bible

The Ten Commandments from the website for Lesson 1.

NOTES

NOTE TO TEACHERS
DISCUSSION: WHEN YOU SEE ITEMS IN ALL CAPS, THEY ARE NOTES TO SHARE WITH YOUR CLASS. (Notes in parentheses are notes and thoughts for the teacher.)

DISCUSSION: NO POWER ON EARTH IS A SUITABLE SUBSTITUTE FOR GOD'S POWER IN OUR LIVES. GOD HAS POWER OVER ALL!

Prayer: *Heavenly Father, we pray for those who fight against you and are stubborn in their ways. Touch their hearts, Lord, and allow them to see who you are. May we help them see your love and kindness by letting you shine through us. Amen.*

Lesson 3 (Nahum 3:8-13)

Takeaway: Thebes and Nineveh put their trust in weapons and war.

Takeaway: History would show that these were inadequate.

DISCUSSION: WE DON'T HAVE TO ALWAYS LEARN THROUGH PERSONAL EXPERIENCE; INSTEAD, WE CAN LEARN THE LESSONS HISTORY HAS ALREADY TAUGHT US. WE DON'T HAVE TO REPEAT THE SAME MISTAKES AS OTHERS. WE CAN PUT OUR TRUST IN GOD ABOVE ALL ELSE.

Prayer: *God, we hear the saying, "They have to make their own mistakes in life in order to learn." Help us rise above that and learn from the lessons of the Bible. You have given them to us as a personal guide in life. May we put them as our top priority and allow your guidance to be our first and only lead in life. Amen.*

Lesson 4 (Nahum 3:14-19)

Takeaway: All the nations hated to be ruled by the merciless people of Nineveh, but the nations wanted to be powerful, wealthy, and prestigious like them, so they developed a friendship with them.

Takeaway: God powerfully destroyed the Assyrian Empire because of their love of power.

> **DISCUSSION:** WE DON'T LIKE BEING TOLD WHAT TO DO BY OTHERS AND DEEP DOWN WOULD LIKE TO HAVE POWER OVER THEM INSTEAD. CHOOSE TO WORK AND LIVE FOR GOD ACCORDING TO HIS PLAN AND LET HIS POWER BE GLORIFIED. WHAT COMMANDMENTS ARE GOOD REMINDERS FOR US OF THIS? (One and four.)

Prayer: *Lord God, we look to you for answers and know that you want us to respect our parents, teachers, and other leaders in our lives. May we allow your power to work in us as we listen and learn from those who you have put in our lives to teach us. Help us continue to put you and your lessons first on our walk here on earth. Amen.*

MORNING BIBLE STUDY

3RD GRADE - HABAKKUK

There is no running from God!

Saying no to God quickly leads to disaster. Saying yes brings a new understanding of God and His purpose in the world.

Habakkuk lived in Judah during the reign of Jehoiakim. He prophesied between the fall of Nineveh and the Babylonian invasion of Judah. With Assyria in disarray, Babylon was becoming the dominant world power. This book records the prophet's dialogue with God concerning the questions, "Why does God often seem indifferent in the face of evil?" and "Why do evil people seem to go unpunished?" While other prophetic books brought God's word to the people, this book brought people's questions to God. Allow the book of Habakkuk to help you understand God and His ways better.

HABAKKUK WEEK 20

HABAKKUK 1

Lesson 1 (Habakkuk 1:1-4)

Takeaway: Habakkuk was upset about all the violence and corruption he saw around him and poured out his heart to God.

Takeaway: God has a long-range plan and purpose and is doing right, even when things don't quite make sense.

> **DISCUSSION:** DON'T LET THE WORRIES OF THE WORLD CAUSE YOU TO DOUBT GOD AND TURN AGAINST HIM. GOD ALWAYS HAS A PLAN AND WILL FOLLOW THROUGH WITH ALL THE PROMISES HE HAS MADE.

Prayer: *Lord, we put our trust in you always. Help us continue to trust when things are not feeling safe or right in this world. We know that you are still in control and will protect us for your purposes. Amen.*

Lesson 2 (Habakkuk 1:5-11)

Takeaway: God assured Habakkuk that He would do amazing acts that would astound him.

Takeaway: We must be truly humble and willing to accept God's answers and timing with things.

> **DISCUSSION:** YOU WON'T COMPLETELY UNDERSTAND WHY YOUR PARENTS DO SOME OF THE THINGS THAT THEY DO UNTIL YOU BECOME A PARENT. EVERYTHING STARTS TO MAKE SENSE WHEN YOU ARE IN THEIR ROLE. YOU MUST

MATERIALS
The Bible

NOTES

NOTE TO TEACHERS
DISCUSSION: WHEN YOU SEE ITEMS IN ALL CAPS, THEY ARE NOTES TO SHARE WITH YOUR CLASS. (Notes in parentheses are notes and thoughts for the teacher.)

> TRUST IN YOUR PARENTS AND GOD. BE PATIENT, IT WILL
> ALL MAKE SENSE ONE DAY.

Prayer: *Heavenly Father, we ask for you to help us continue to trust in our parents and other leaders in life that sometimes don't make sense to us. Help us understand that they want what is best for us, and we need to allow them to direct us in whatever way they feel is necessary. May we listen, respect, and do as they ask. Amen.*

Lesson 3 (Habakkuk 1:5-11)

Takeaway: God's people would see a series of unbelievable events: 1. The independent prosperous kingdom of Judah would be taken over. 2. Egypt would be crushed almost overnight. 3. Nineveh would be so completely ransacked that people would forget it ever existed. 4. The wicked Babylonians would rise to power under God's plan.

Takeaway: God keeps His promises by fulfilling the prophesies.

> **DISCUSSION:** AS A CHRISTIAN, WE SHOULD ASK GOD HOW WE CAN SERVE HIM AND HIS PLAN THROUGH DIFFICULT TIMES. WORK FOR GOD THROUGH MESSY TIMES RATHER THAN LETTING THE MESS AFFECT YOU. HOW CAN WE DO THIS? (Pray, be proactive with things, follow our leaders, be an example for others, help others trust in God and our leaders' work.)

Prayer: *God, we know that things can get crazy in life sometimes, and we may wonder where you are. Help us step up to whatever you need us to do even if it seems small, like respecting those who lead us. We want to help others by setting a good example. Thank you for your protection and work here on earth. Amen.*

• •

Lesson 4 (Habakkuk 1: 12-17)

Takeaway: Habakkuk was horrified that God would use a nation even more wicked than Judah to punish it.

Takeaway: The Babylonians did not know that God was using them to return Judah to Him, and their pride would be their downfall in God's plan.

> **DISCUSSION:** GOD MAY USE WHATEVER UNUSUAL CIRCUMSTANCES HE CHOOSES TO CORRECT OR PUNISH THE SIN. WHEN WE SIN, OUR PUNISHMENT HELPS US LEARN AND DO BETTER. HOW CAN WE COMPLAIN ABOUT HOW GOD GOES ABOUT HANDLING IT? GOD ALWAYS KNOWS BEST.

Prayer: *Lord, we give you this day and all our days to teach us and be part of your plan here on earth. Whatever you need from us, we are willing to do, even if it doesn't always make sense to us. May you guide us and give us the strength, words, and actions we need to take. Amen.*

HABAKKUK WEEK 21

HABAKKUK 2

Lesson 1 (Habakkuk 2:1-4)

Takeaway: Habakkuk uses the watchman and rampart (watchtower) to show a picture of how he is patiently waiting and watching for God's response.

Takeaway: The watchtowers were usually built on the city walls so that watchmen could see enemies or messengers approaching their city from a distance.

> **DISCUSSION:** HABAKKUK SHOWED GOD THAT HE HAD THE RIGHT ATTITUDE AND WAS READY TO RECEIVE HIS MESSAGE. WHAT DOES YOUR ATTITUDE SHOW GOD? ARE YOU READY TO RECEIVE HIS MESSAGE AND WORK FOR HIS KINGDOM? (For me, I see myself clocking in each morning to go to work as soon as I get out of bed, doing God's work. I clock out when I hit the pillow after I have praised Him for the ten ways I saw Him in my day.)

Prayer: *Lord, we want to have a good attitude each day so that we can listen to what you put on our hearts and go out and do your work in our school, community, and home. Set us straight, Lord, when we have a bad attitude and put us back on the right path. May we learn to be your disciples with attitudes that shine like gold. Amen.*

MATERIALS
The Bible

OTHER RESOURCES
Romans 1:17, Galatians 3:11, and Hebrews 10:38 for Lesson 2.

NOTE TO TEACHERS
DISCUSSION: WHEN YOU SEE ITEMS IN ALL CAPS, THEY ARE NOTES TO SHARE WITH YOUR CLASS. (Notes in parentheses are notes and thoughts for the teacher.)

63

● ●

Lesson 2 (Habakkuk 2:1-4)

Takeaway: Verse four inspires many Christians and is often quoted throughout the Bible. (See Romans 1:17, Galatians 3:11, and Hebrews 10:38.)

Takeaway: This verse gives hope for those who are living through difficult times.

> **DISCUSSION:** WE MUST TRUST THAT GOD DIRECTS ALL THINGS ACCORDING TO HIS PURPOSES. TO HAVE FAITH IS TO TRUST IN THE LORD.

Prayer: *Heavenly Father, we turn to you in good times and praise you for all your glory. We also come to you in hard times, seeking comfort and courage to follow through with whatever you ask of us. Help us continue to turn to you and help others. We know you are behind all things in life. Amen.*

Lesson 3 (Habakkuk 2:5-20)

Takeaway: Money is not evil, but God condemns loving it.

Takeaway: God doesn't want the love of money to come before Him.

> **DISCUSSION:** WE SHOULD NEVER LET THE LOVE OF MONEY TAKE THE PLACE OF GOD, FAMILY, OR FRIENDS. THE LOVE OF MONEY IS A WORLDLY THING, WHILE THE OTHERS ARE GIFTS FROM GOD.

Prayer: *God, we are so thankful for our relationship with you and for those you have put in our lives. May we never take anything or anyone for granted. You are so gracious. Amen.*

Lesson 4 (Habakkuk 2:5-20)

Takeaway: Having an idol is not just bowing down to a statue or a famous singer. If we say we worship God but allow other things to be more important than Him, then they have become an idol in our lives.

Takeaway: When we worship God, we trust in what He has created and His power over all things.

DISCUSSION: DO YOU PUT YOUR TRUST IN GOD WITH EVERYTHING THAT YOU DO? DO YOU PUT HIM BEFORE ALL OTHER THINGS IN LIFE? WHAT ARE SOME AREAS THAT YOU MIGHT NEED TO WORK ON? (You can share an example of an area from your life. For me, I need to make family more of a priority in my life by spending more one-on-one time with my kids. I also need to spend more time listening to God in prayer and taking in the beauty of His creations by walking more.)

Prayer: *Lord, we take time today to reprioritize the things we find important in our lives and to slow down, listen, and appreciate more. Help us hear what you ask us to do and make a change to grow closer to you in our faith. Amen.*

HABAKKUK WEEK 22

HABAKKUK 3

Lesson 1 (Habakkuk 3:1-2)

Takeaway: Habakkuk knew that when God disciplined Judah, it would not be pleasant.

Takeaway: Habakkuk asked God for mercy and accepted the discipline that was coming instead of trying to escape it.

> **DISCUSSION:** GOD DISCIPLINES WITH LOVE TO BRING HIS CHILDREN BACK TO HIM. (Hebrews 12:5) ASK GOD TO HELP YOU CHANGE AND ACCEPT THE DISCIPLINE THAT MIGHT GO WITH IT.

Prayer: *Lord God, we know that it is so hard to change some things when we are set in our ways. If we dishonor you, we ask for your help to make the needed changes. Help us be strong and ready for whatever you bring our way. Amen.*

Lesson 2 (Habakkuk 3:3-16)

Takeaway: Habakkuk paints the picture of God's deliverance of His people from Egypt, as told in Exodus 14.

Takeaway: God is not only creative in His work, as seen in the beauty of this world, but He is also righteous and just.

MATERIALS
The Bible

OTHER RESOURCES
Hebrews 12:5 for Lesson 1.

NOTE TO TEACHERS
DISCUSSION: WHEN YOU SEE ITEMS IN ALL CAPS, THEY ARE NOTES TO SHARE WITH YOUR CLASS. (Notes in parentheses are notes and thoughts for the teacher.)

• •

> **DISCUSSION:** WE CAN'T JUST BE IN AWE OF GOD'S CREATION AND POWER. WE NEED TO LEARN HOW TO OBEY AND LIVE FOR HIM. HOW CAN WE DO THIS? (By following the Ten Commandments, accepting discipline when we have done wrong and disobeyed, praying for God's guidance.)

Prayer: *Heavenly Father, we know of so many ways you helped your people in the Bible and showed us your awesome power. Help us be faithful disciples and learn from our mistakes so others can also learn from them. May we be your light here on earth. Amen.*

Lesson 3 (Habakkuk 3:17-19)

Takeaway: Even though the crops would fail and animals would die, Habakkuk still rejoiced in the Lord.

Takeaway: Habakkuk lived by faith in God and the strength God gave him, rather than being controlled by the events happening around him.

> **DISCUSSION:** LOOK TO GOD FOR EVERYTHING AND FIND STRENGTH AND HAPPINESS! WHY CAN'T WE COUNT ON WORLDLY THINGS TO GIVE US STRENGTH AND HAPPINESS? (No one is as strong as God. Worldly things are only temporary and change, while God never does.)

Prayer: *God, we turn to you for strength. Joy fills our hearts the more we know you. May we communicate with you daily and always listen to you in our hearts. We find peace and comfort in our faith with you. Amen.*

Lesson 4 (Habakkuk 3:17-19)

Takeaway: God gives us strength and confidence when we choose to follow Him.

Takeaway: At the right time, God will take away all evil in the world.

> **DISCUSSION:** WE DON'T SEE ALL THAT GOD IS DOING AND WILL DO IN THE FUTURE, BUT WE KNOW THAT HE IS OUR GOD AND WILL DO WHAT IS RIGHT!

Prayer: *God, we trust in you and all that you do and will do in the future. We wait patiently for your guidance and to discover our calling in life as we follow you here on hear. We give it all to you in your timing. Amen.*

MORNING BIBLE STUDY

3RD GRADE - THE BOOK OF ZEPHANIAH

There is no running from God!
Saying no to God quickly leads to disaster. Saying yes brings a
new understanding of God and His purpose in the world.

The book of Zephaniah teaches about the day of judgment and what it looks like to no longer care about God. This book can help you listen better to your Lord and trust in His guidance.

Judah will show no sorrow for its sins and will live for security and wealth. Material comforts will challenge your relationship with God. You must work hard to put God first, above all else. Money won't get us to Heaven, only Jesus does. God will restore His people and give them hope. We, too, are given this hope through our faith, when we turn to His Son Jesus.

ZEPHANIAH WEEK 23

ZEPHANIAH I

Lesson 1 (Zephaniah 1:1-4)

Takeaway: The Israelites failed to rid the land of its pagan inhabitants when they arrived in the Promised Land as God had commanded them.

Takeaway: Gradually, the Israelites began to worship the Canaanite gods. Baal was the god of strength and fertility.

> **DISCUSSION:** GOD WAS ANGRY WITH HIS PEOPLE FOR TURNING FROM HIM AND TO BAAL INSTEAD. WHY WOULD HIS PEOPLE DO THIS? (Baal was something they could see and touch; they were tired of waiting on God's timing for things, so they took it into their own hands; they were following their peers …)

Prayer: *Lord God, we ask for strength to always put you first in our lives. When we are tempted to allow worldly things to come before you, help us feel your love in our hearts and remind us of all your glory. May we see the value of the faith and joy that comes from following you. Help us stay strong on our journey in life. Amen.*

Lesson 2 (Zephaniah 1:5-6)

Takeaway: The people began worshiping the Lord and all the other gods of the land.

MATERIALS
The Bible

OTHER RESOURCES

Leviticus 18:21 and 20:5 and Exodus 20:1-5 for Lesson 2.

Revelation 20:12-15 for Lesson 4.

NOTE TO TEACHERS
DISCUSSION: WHEN YOU SEE ITEMS IN ALL CAPS, THEY ARE NOTES TO SHARE WITH YOUR CLASS. (Notes in parentheses are notes and thoughts for the teacher.)

• •

Takeaway: One of these other gods was Milcom (Molech), the god of the Ammonites, which included child sacrifice as part of the worship.

> **DISCUSSION:** THE ISRAELITES HAD BEEN WARNED ABOUT WORSHIPPING FALSE GODS SINCE THE TIME OF MOSES. (Leviticus 18:21 and 20:5) GOD COMMANDS THAT WE WORSHIP HIM ALONE. (See Exodus 20:1-5 and commandment number one.)

Prayer: *Again and again, Lord, we hear of people not putting you first in their lives and worshiping other gods. Help us learn from their mistakes and see how silly it is to think that anything could possibly be above you in our lives. May we praise you daily and help others see the importance of putting you above all. Amen.*

Lesson 3 (Zephaniah 1:7-13)

Takeaway: A great number of people died at the hands of the Babylonians on their day of judgment.

Takeaway: The prophets saw these predictions as future events but could not see when they would take place.

> **DISCUSSION:** THESE EVENTS SHOW US WHAT OUR FUTURE HOLDS WHEN JESUS RETURNS TO THIS EARTH. THERE WILL BE ANOTHER JUDGMENT DAY. WHAT DO YOU THINK ABOUT THIS? (Scary? Excited? Don't want to leave the world?)

Prayer: *Heavenly Father, we want to be prepared for the coming of your Son Jesus Christ on the day He returns. Help us strengthen our faith and be ready to greet Him with open arms and hearts! We look forward to being with you both in Heaven. Amen.*

Lesson 4 (Zephaniah 1:14-18)

Takeaway: The "great day of the Lord" was near, and the Babylonians would soon destroy Jerusalem.

Takeaway: We will also have the day of the Lord when Jesus returns, as told in Revelation 20:12-15.

> **DISCUSSION:** TO PREPARE FOR HIS RETURN: RECOGNIZE YOUR SINS, CONFESS THEM TO GOD, KNOW THAT YOU CANNOT SAVE YOURSELF, ONLY GOD CAN!

Prayer: *Lord, we offer up our sins and ask that you forgive us as we try to change our ways by turning the other direction. Help us learn from our mistakes, forgive one another, and know that we are nothing without you. May we spend our time praising you for all your glory and thanking you for our blessings. Amen.*

ZEPHANIAH WEEK 24

ZEPHANIAH 2

Lesson 1 (Zephaniah 2:1-3)

Takeaway: There was still time for the people to turn away from their sins and start obeying God.

Takeaway: The prophets of the Old Testament announced news of destruction, but they also offered a way to escape and be protected. (Micah 6:8)

> **DISCUSSION:** JUST AS GOD'S JUDGMENT AGAINST JUDAH CAME WITH PLENTY OF WARNING, GOD ALSO WARNS US CONCERNING THE FINAL DAY OF JUDGMENT. WE MUST PRAY FOR THE FORGIVENESS OF OUR SINS, ASK FOR GOD TO BRING US INTO HIS HEAVENLY KINGDOM, AND OBEY HIM WHILE WE ARE HERE ON EARTH. GOD GAVE US THE BIBLE TO WARN AND INSTRUCT US. HOW CAN YOU HELP OTHERS WITH THESE MESSAGES FROM GOD? (Tell them about what we are learning in the Bible, encourage them to read with you, pray for them.)

Prayer: *Lord, help us be faithful to the lessons in your Word and help others know you and have an opportunity to build a relationship with you. We know we can always pray for those who don't believe or criticize us for our beliefs, and so we ask that you help them, Lord, seek the truth and find you someday. May they rest in the comforts of knowing you. Amen.*

MATERIALS
The Bible

OTHER RESOURCES

Micah 6:8 for Lesson 1.

Genesis 17:4-8 for Lesson 2.

NOTE TO TEACHERS
DISCUSSION: WHEN YOU SEE ITEMS IN ALL CAPS, THEY ARE NOTES TO SHARE WITH YOUR CLASS. (Notes in parentheses are notes and thoughts for the teacher.)

Lesson 2 (Zephaniah 2:4-7)

Takeaway: Although God said He would destroy Judah, He also kept His covenant with Abraham and promised to save some. (Genesis 17:4-8)

Takeaway: God is holy and cannot allow sin to continue, but He also will not stay angry forever and is faithful to His promises.

> **DISCUSSION:** GOD LOVES HIS CHILDREN AND ALWAYS WANTS WHAT'S BEST FOR THEM. DO YOU LOOK FOR THE GOOD IN OTHERS AND FORGIVE?

Prayer: *Heavenly Father, we ask you to lay upon our hearts anyone you feel we have not given a fair chance to or that we may have some hatred toward. Help us see the good in them as your image-bearers so that we can focus on forgiving them and working on our relationship with them. May we love everyone as your Son Jesus does. Amen.*

Lesson 3 (Zephaniah 2:8-11)

Takeaway: Other nations insulted Judah, but God reminded them that they would be punished for their pride.

Takeaway: The whole world seemed to mock God and those who had faith in Him.

> **DISCUSSION:** GOD ALWAYS HEARS THE PRAYERS OF HIS CHILDREN AND WILL ANSWER THEM. HE ALSO CARRIES OUT JUSTICE IN HIS OWN TIMING. HAVE TRUST IN GOD'S WORK IN YOUR LIFE AND IN THOSE WHO LAUGH AT YOU.

Prayer: *God, we pray for those who don't have faith in you and live their lives without following your commands. May they understand the true joy of loving their neighbors and putting you first in their lives. We pray for their souls and those who are hurt by their selfishness and ways of living. Amen.*

Lesson 4 (Zephaniah 2:12-15)

Takeaway: Nineveh was a place similar to Paris or New York. It had great libraries, buildings, and beautiful gardens.

Takeaway: The city wall was sixty miles long, one hundred feet high, and over thirty feet wide with 1,500 towers within it.

> **DISCUSSION:** NINEVEH HAD BECOME AS DESOLATE AND DRY AS THE WILDERNESS, JUST AS ZEPHANIAH SAID IT WOULD. OUR LIVES ON THIS EARTH ARE ONLY TEMPORARY. DON'T FALL IN LOVE WITH THE WORLDLY BEAUTY, BUT RATHER WITH YOUR GOD.

Prayer: *Lord, we are in awe of all that you have created and the talents you have given people to create beauty and comforts for us here on earth. Let us never forget that you are the reason for it all. Know that we would not have the knowledge or talents to design, build, and create as we do without the power of our creator. May we never take that for granted. Amen.*

ZEPHANIAH WEEK 25

ZEPHANIAH 3

Lesson 1 (Zephaniah 3:1-2)

Takeaway: The people pretended to worship God, but they continued to sin in their hearts.

Takeaway: They no longer cared about any consequences for their actions or thoughts.

> **DISCUSSION:** DO YOU KNOW PEOPLE WHO CHOOSE NOT TO LISTEN TO THOSE WHO DISAGREE WITH THEM? PRIDE IS THE ROOT OF THE PROBLEM. IT IS ALWAYS GOOD TO SEE THINGS FROM BOTH SIDES AND THEN DO WHAT JESUS WOULD DO. HOW CAN WE DO THIS? (Decide if it is breaking any of the commandments, loving our neighbors through our decisions, through prayer.)

Prayer: *Lord, we want to be open-minded to all people, yet listen to your guidance in life. Help us listen to others and then make the right choices according to your guidance. We continue to follow you and give you our hearts. Amen.*

Lesson 2 (Zephaniah 3:3-7)

Takeaway: Jerusalem was the religious center of the nation where the temple was located.

Takeaway: Even though people didn't follow God, He was still there.

> **DISCUSSION:** NO MATTER WHAT, GOD IS HERE. HE IS ALWAYS AT WORK AND FOCUSED ON YOUR BEST

MATERIALS

The Bible

NOTES

NOTE TO TEACHERS
DISCUSSION: WHEN YOU SEE ITEMS IN ALL CAPS, THEY ARE NOTES TO SHARE WITH YOUR CLASS. (Notes in parentheses are notes and thoughts for the teacher.)

> INTERESTS. OPEN YOUR EYES TO SEE WHAT HE IS DOING RIGHT NOW AND ASK HIM HOW YOU CAN BE A PART OF HIS WORK.

Prayer: *Heavenly Father, we find comfort in knowing you are always in charge and that you are taking care of us. Let us know in our hearts what it is that you need from us to do our part in your work. We are here to serve and love others as you ask of us. Amen.*

Lesson 3 (Zephaniah 3:8-13)

Takeaway: Verse nine shares how God will unify languages so that all His people will be able to understand each other.

Takeaway: Verses eleven and twelve tell us how God will purify our hearts so that the words from our lips will be pure.

> **DISCUSSION:** IN THE NEW EARTH, THE CONFUSION OF LANGUAGES THAT HAPPENED AT THE TOWER OF BABEL (Genesis 11) WILL BE REVERSED, AND ALL WILL BE ABLE TO WORSHIP HIM TOGETHER. THERE WILL BE NO SELFISHNESS IN HEAVEN EITHER, ONLY WORSHIP AND LOVE.

Prayer: *God, we are so hopeful of your return and cannot wait to take our place in your kingdom. We look forward to meeting you someday and worshiping you in unity and awe. May you open your doors to us when you see us, and may all your people be joined together in love and worship for you. Amen.*

Lesson 4 (Zephaniah 3:12-18)

Takeaway: The Lord will remove His hand of judgment when He comes to live among the people causing great joy.

Takeaway: Zephaniah reminds us that gladness comes when we allow God to be with us.

• •

DISCUSSION: HAPPINESS COMES FROM FOLLOWING GOD'S COMMANDS. WHEN WE DO THIS, GOD'S LOVE MOVES THROUGH US, AND WE FEEL IT IN OUR HEARTS. JUST AS A FAMILY FINDS PEACE WHEN GETTING ALONG AND FOLLOWING THEIR PARENTS, WE FIND PEACE IN OUR HEARTS BY DOING WHAT GOD ASKS OF US AND LOVING OUR NEIGHBORS.

Prayer: *Lord, we thank you for the commandments that you have given us. They teach us right from wrong and how to love one another. Help us follow these at home, school, and in our community, even when we feel no one is looking or knows how we feel inside about something. Clean our hearts and faithfully push us in the right direction, so we can make good choices in life as we follow your path for us. Amen.*

MORNING BIBLE STUDY

3RD GRADE - THE BOOK OF HAGGAI

There is no running from God!
Saying no to God quickly leads to disaster. Saying yes brings a
new understanding of God and His purpose in the world.

In the book of Haggai, people are called to complete the rebuilding of the temple in Jerusalem. As they traveled back to Jerusalem from exile to begin working, they forgot their purpose and brought the work to a standstill. Haggai calls them back to God's values, and the temple was completed.

How we spend our time, money, and talent shows us our values and priorities. Let the book of Haggai help you claim God as the number one priority in your life.

HAGGAI WEEK 26

HAGGAI I

Lesson 1 (Haggai 1:1-6)

Takeaway: The broken temple showed the relationship between Judah and God.

Takeaway: The people put their energies into making their own homes beautiful, instead of rebuilding the temple for God.

> **DISCUSSION:** NO MATTER HOW HARD A PERSON WORKS, THEY WILL HAVE LESS IF THEY IGNORE THEIR SPIRITUAL LIFE. IF YOU PUT GOD FIRST, HE WILL PROVIDE FOR YOUR NEEDS AND GIVE YOU SATISFACTION AND COMFORT IN YOUR HEART. WITHOUT HIM IN OUR LIVES, IT LEADS TO DESTRUCTION. WHAT DO YOU THINK THIS MEANS? (You can't truly be happy without God; material things don't bring happiness; life is not about success and money, it's about love.)

Prayer: *Lord God, we ask you to continue to work in our hearts and in the hearts of others, reminding us of the importance of our relationships and the way we love and care for people. May we not allow material things to run our lives or put meaningless things in front of you, God. Let our love for you and others be our focus. Amen.*

Lesson 2 (Haggai 1:7-11)

Takeaway: God withheld His blessing because people were no longer putting Him first in their lives, as Moses had once predicted would happen. (Deuteronomy 28:38-45)

MATERIALS
The Bible

OTHER RESOURCES
Deuteronomy 28:38-45 for Lesson 2.

NOTE TO TEACHERS
DISCUSSION: WHEN YOU SEE ITEMS IN ALL CAPS, THEY ARE NOTES TO SHARE WITH YOUR CLASS. (Notes in parentheses are notes and thoughts for the teacher.)

Takeaway: Judah was confusing their priorities of God, family, and occupation.

> **DISCUSSION:** IS HAVING FREE TIME IN YOUR LIFE OR BEING ABLE TO BUY SOMETHING MORE IMPORTANT TO YOU THAN YOUR TIME WITH GOD? WHERE IS GOD ON YOUR LIST OF PRIORITIES? LET'S TAKE TIME TODAY TO SEE IF THERE IS AN AREA WE NEED TO WORK ON TO PUT GOD FIRST AGAIN.

Prayer: *God, we ask you to lay on our hearts anything that is getting in our way of putting you first. (PAUSE.) Help us be aware of that and find a way to put you back on top. We know you are most deserving and should always be above everything else. May we keep family right below you and love them as you ask. Amen.*

Lesson 3 (Haggai 1:12-15)

Takeaway: The people responded to Haggai's first message to begin rebuilding the temple twenty-three days later.

Takeaway: This was not a normal thing for people to do so quickly after hearing a prophet's message.

> **DISCUSSION:** HAVE YOU EVER MADE A DECISION TO MAKE A CHANGE OR START DOING SOMETHING WHILE YOU ARE AT SCHOOL OR CHURCH, THEN CHANGE YOUR MIND BY THE TIME YOU GET HOME, AND DON'T DO IT? THESE PEOPLE PUT THEIR WORDS INTO ACTION! WHEN GOD CALLS US, WE NEED TO DO THE SAME!

Prayer: *Help us, God, hear your voice in our hearts and take the steps forward that we need to take to do your work. Sometimes it can be challenging, but don't allow us to procrastinate or be afraid of failure. We learn from failure and grow stronger from it. May we always put our words into action for you. Amen.*

Lesson 4 (Haggai 1)

Takeaway: Haggai had encouraged the people to rebuild the temple despite all the hostile neighbors discouraging them.

Takeaway: Haggai's message motivated them to work.

> **DISCUSSION:** DO YOU KNOW SOMEONE IN YOUR LIFE WHO MOTIVATES YOU LIKE THIS? IT'S IMPORTANT TO BE AROUND PEOPLE WHO LIFT YOU UP AND THOSE WHO POINT YOU TO THE LORD. BE THAT PERSON FOR OTHERS, TOO. LOOK FOR GOD'S BLESSING IN EVERYTHING AND POINT OTHERS IN THAT DIRECTION.

Prayer: *Heavenly Father, help us be the sunlight for others and draw ourselves closer to those who give us the light we need. As you guide us on our path, may we stay strong with the help of others to lean on, who can also lean on us for support and encouragement because of our faith in you. Amen.*

HAGGAI WEEK 27

HAGGAI 2

Lesson 1 (Haggai 2:1-5)

Takeaway: Haggai's second message encouraged the people to work hard and be strong as they focused on the work they needed to do now, rather than focusing on the past.

Takeaway: The older people remembered the beauty of the temple before it was destroyed and were discouraged with how the rebuilding looked.

> **DISCUSSION:** THE MOST IMPORTANT PART OF THE TEMPLE IS THE PRESENCE OF GOD. SOME FIVE HUNDRED YEARS LATER, JESUS CHRIST WOULD WALK THROUGH THIS VERY TEMPLE. GOD'S SPIRIT IS IN US AND WILL HELP US DO THE WORK HE HAS PLANNED FOR US. JUST AS GOD WAS WITH THEM, HE IS WITH YOU.

Prayer: *Lord, we feel your presence in our lives and the love you have given us in our hearts to do your work. Help us stay focused and strong even through the hard times. May we never focus on the past but look to the future and all that you have for us to do and will bless us with. Amen.*

Lesson 2 (Haggai 2:6-9)

> **DISCUSSION:** THE "DESIRE OF ALL NATIONS" COULD HAVE TWO POSSIBLE MEANINGS:

Takeaway: It could be Jesus who would fill it with His peace and glory.

MATERIALS
The Bible

OTHER RESOURCES

The 10 Ways I Saw God Today from the website for Lesson 3.

Matthew 1:12-16 and Ephesians 1:4 for Lesson 4.

NOTE TO TEACHERS
DISCUSSION: WHEN YOU SEE ITEMS IN ALL CAPS, THEY ARE NOTES TO SHARE WITH YOUR CLASS. (Notes in parentheses are notes and thoughts for the teacher.)

Takeaway: It could be all the riches that would flow into the temple as offerings.

> **DISCUSSION:** GOD WANTED THE TEMPLE REBUILT, BUT HE WANTED THE WORK DONE BY HUMAN HANDS. GOD CHOOSES TO USE PEOPLE AND PROVIDES THE RESOURCES TO THOSE WITH WILLING HANDS. ARE YOUR HANDS READY AND WILLING TO DO HIS WORK?

Prayer: *Heavenly Father, we trust in you and want to be your helpers. Help us stay on track and be willing to work hard to help you accomplish your plans. May we stay faithful and strong. Amen.*

Lesson 3 (Haggai 2:10-19)

Takeaway: For many years, the grain had yielded only 50 percent of what was expected, and the winepress even worse than that.

Takeaway: God immediately blessed the people for laying the temple's foundation. He didn't wait for them to complete the project; instead, He sent encouragement and approval of their obedience.

> **DISCUSSION:** GOD ALSO SENDS US BLESSINGS. NOTICE THE BLESSINGS HE SENDS YOU WHEN YOU ARE DOING HIS WORK. TAKE NOTE OF THEM AND TAKE TIME TO THANK HIM.

Prayer: *God, we know that our lives are full of blessings. You provide us with all that we need. May we take the time to thank you and take note of all that you do for us. Help us make this a daily habit in our lives. Amen.*

Lesson 4 (Haggai 2:20-23)

Takeaway: Haggai addressed his final message to Zerubbabel, the governor of Judah, chosen by God.

Takeaway: God reaffirmed His promise of a Messiah through the line of David. (Matthew 1:12-16)

> **DISCUSSION:** GOD HAS CHOSEN EACH OF US AS IT IS SAID IN EPHESIANS 1:4. WHEN YOU FEEL WORRIED OR WANT TO QUIT SOMETHING, REMEMBER THAT GOD HAS CHOSEN YOU. GOD WILL GIVE YOU STRENGTH AND GUIDANCE THROUGHOUT YOUR LIFE.

Prayer: *Lord, we are in awe of all that you are. We are so blessed to be your children and have you work through us. May we never doubt what you have in store for us and move forward always with strength, love, and a heart to do your work. Amen.*

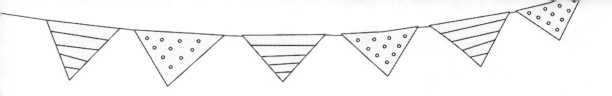

MORNING BIBLE STUDY

3RD GRADE - ZECHARIAH

There is no running from God!

Saying no to God quickly leads to disaster. Saying yes brings a new understanding of God and His purpose in the world.

Zechariah gives hope to God's people by revealing God's plan of the Messiah. In this book, you will see the details of Christ's life written five hundred years before their fulfillment.

God keeps His promise, and Zechariah's visions provide hope for the people. He describes eight visions that come to him at night to encourage the people to continue rebuilding the temple.

We, too, should be encouraged by the return of Christ, who will reign forever and ever.

ZECHARIAH WEEK 28

ZECHARIAH 1

Lesson 1 (Zechariah 1:1-6)

Takeaway: Zechariah was a prophet and a priest who gave his first message to the people two months after Haggai's first message.

Takeaway: He was encouraging the people to continue to rebuild the temple, as the reconstruction had stopped for nearly ten years.

> **DISCUSSION:** IT IS NEVER TOO LATE TO START FOLLOWING GOD. DON'T EVER GIVE UP ON THOSE AROUND YOU THAT YOU FEEL WILL NEVER CHANGE. CONTINUE TO LOVE THEM, SHOW THEM CHRIST IN YOUR HEART, AND ALLOW GOD TO DO THE WORK ON HIS TIMING. GIVE AN EXAMPLE OF WHEN YOU HAVE WAITED ON GOD'S TIMING. (For me, my husband didn't attend church the first year or two of our daughter's life. I would ask him every week if he would like to go to church with us. He would say no, but I never gave up on him. Eventually, he said yes and has attended ever since. The power of God's timing and the wonderful advice by another Christian taught me to never give up on someone.)

Prayer: *Lord, we know that there are people in this world who have suffered and have turned away from you. Some people have never allowed themselves to experience your love because of how they were raised. We pray for their hearts and ask you to stay close to them. May we help in any way that you need so that all can enter into your kingdom and know you. Amen.*

MATERIALS
The Bible

NOTES

NOTE TO TEACHERS
DISCUSSION: WHEN YOU SEE ITEMS IN ALL CAPS, THEY ARE NOTES TO SHARE WITH YOUR CLASS. (Notes in parentheses are notes and thoughts for the teacher.)

Lesson 2 (Zechariah 1:1-6)

Takeaway: When someone says, "Like father, like son," they imply that the child turned out just like their parent. But, God warns us not to do that.

Takeaway: God warns Israel to learn from their father's mistakes and the punishment they received and choose to do things differently.

DISCUSSION: WE ARE RESPONSIBLE FOR OUR OWN ACTIONS AND ARE FREE TO CHOOSE TO FOLLOW GOD AND HIS COMMANDMENTS. LEARN FROM OTHERS AND MAKE WISE CHOICES IN LIFE. DOES ANYONE HAVE AN EXAMPLE THEY WOULD LIKE TO SHARE? (Examples: a friend receives a consequence at school for something they did, someone hurts another because of their actions, someone doesn't finish school and has trouble finding a job.)

Prayer: *Lord God, we thank you for the Bible and all the lessons it gives us. Help us learn from these lessons and see how you are guiding us through life. Thank you for the good examples of others and the people who love us and help us follow you. Amen.*

. . . .

Lesson 3 (Zechariah 1:7-17)

Takeaway: Zechariah sees messengers reporting to God how the nations around Judah are living in sin with no worries.

Takeaway: Israel wants to know why God isn't punishing them?

> **DISCUSSION:** GOD BRINGS JUDGMENT IN HIS OWN TIMING. WE MUST BE PATIENT AND KNOW THAT OTHERS WILL NOT GET AWAY WITH EVILNESS FOREVER. THINGS CATCH UP WITH PEOPLE, AND THE TRUTH ALWAYS SHINES. GOD IS BEHIND EVERYTHING. GIVE AN EXAMPLE OF THIS HAPPENING IN YOUR LIFE. (For me, a leader in a school system I was involved with would be kind to people to their face and then make up things about them behind their back to make themselves look better. I prayed for them and tried to confront them with their sin but was pushed away and talked about behind my back as well to keep others from listening to me. Eventually, when they applied for a higher position within the school, they were not hired and so left to go somewhere else because everything had caught up with them. People higher than them saw the truth. It didn't turn them to Christ, but they hopefully learned from their past mistakes and did differently at the next school.)

Prayer: *Heavenly Father, we pray for those who do not know you or listen to your commands. Help them see the yuck inside the things they are doing and choose to follow a better path with you as their guide. May we be there to do whatever you need to help them on their new path in life. Amen.*

Lesson 4 (Zechariah 1:18-21)

Takeaway: The four horns Zechariah sees represent the four world powers that scattered all the people of Judah and Israel.

Takeaway: God will destroy these nations once He feels they have carried out His will of punishing His people.

> **DISCUSSION:** GOD ALWAYS DOES WHAT HE PROMISES. THINGS HAPPEN AS PART OF GOD'S PLAN.

Prayer: *Help us, God, be patient and always trust in your work. Sometimes, we struggle because it doesn't make sense to us. Remind us to continue to pray and believe in the outcome of your plans. You hold all things in your hands and know what is best. Amen.*

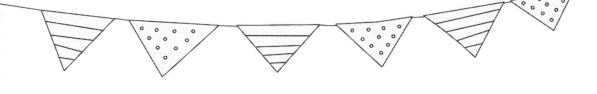

ZECHARIAH WEEK 29

ZECHARIAH 2-3

Lesson 1 (Zechariah 2:1-13)

Takeaway: Zechariah has a vision of a man measuring the city of Jerusalem.

Takeaway: One day, the city will be full of people with God all around it like a wall.

> **DISCUSSION:** GOD WILL KEEP THE PROMISE HE MADE TO PROTECT THE PEOPLE AND RESTORE JERUSALEM.

Prayer: *Lord, it is important that we move forward in life and always trust in your way. Even when things don't look so good for us or we don't understand the future, we must trust you and keep going as your disciples. May we be faithful to your tasks. Amen.*

Lesson 2 (Zechariah 2:1-13)

Takeaway: There were many Israelites who didn't return to Jerusalem because they enjoyed the security and wealth Babylon offered them.

Takeaway: Zechariah instructed them to leave their selfish ways behind so they wouldn't forget their spiritual priorities. He warned them that Babylon would be destroyed. Many rejected his warnings and remained in Babylon.

MATERIALS
The Bible

OTHER RESOURCES

Matthew 25:34-46 for Lesson 2.

Ephesians 4:24 and 1 John 1:9 for Lesson 3.

NOTE TO TEACHERS
DISCUSSION: WHEN YOU SEE ITEMS IN ALL CAPS, THEY ARE NOTES TO SHARE WITH YOUR CLASS. (Notes in parentheses are notes and thoughts for the teacher.)

• •

> **DISCUSSION:** GOD LOVES ALL HIS CHILDREN. THEY WERE ALL WARNED AND HAD THE OPPORTUNITY TO CHOOSE HIM AND LEAVE BABYLON. WE HAVE THE SAME CHOICE TODAY, TO EITHER FOLLOW GOD OR NOT. WE SHOULD CHOOSE TO HELP OTHERS AND TREAT THEM WITH LOVE AND RESPECT. THE WAY WE LOVE OTHERS IS A REFLECTION OF HOW WE LOVE OUR LORD. WHAT DO YOU THINK ABOUT THAT? (Matthew 25:34-46) (How we treat others reflects our relationship with God. We should always think, "What would Jesus do?" Our actions need to be different than those who don't believe.)

Prayer: *Heavenly Father, we turn to you for guidance and strength. Help us always treat those around us with a loving heart focused on you. May we allow others to see our love for you through our actions and our hearts. Amen.*

Lesson 3 (Zechariah 3:1-10)

Takeaway: Zechariah sees the high priest Joshua standing before God in filthy clothes.

Takeaway: Joshua's filthy clothes are exchanged for clean garments when God rejects Satan's accusations against him.

> **DISCUSSION:** GOD HAS TAKEN OUR GARMENTS OF SIN AND REPLACED THEM WITH HIS RIGHTEOUSNESS. (Ephesians 4:24 and 1 John 1:9) WE MUST PUT THE PAST BEHIND US AND HEAD INTO A NEW DIRECTION GUIDED BY THE HOLY SPIRIT.

Prayer: *God, we pray for the strength to defeat the temptations of this life. Help us commit to a new direction, away from sin. Guide us and lead us on that path. Amen.*

Lesson 4 (Zechariah 3:1-10)

Takeaway: There wasn't any priesthood for the Israelites during the time of exile.

Takeaway: In Zechariah's vision, Joshua is the new high priest. One of his duties was to offer a sacrifice on the **Day of Atonement**.

- ◆ *Day of Atonement* – The one day of the year on which the high priest went into the Most Holy Place in the Tabernacle and offered the blood from the sacrifices for his sins and the sins of the people.

DISCUSSION: JESUS WAS THE HIGH PRIEST WHO OFFERED HIMSELF AS THE FINAL SACRIFICE TO ATONE FOR OUR SINS. WE CANNOT REMOVE SIN WITH OUR OWN EFFORTS. WE MUST ALLOW GOD TO REMOVE THEM THROUGH CHRIST. HOW DO WE DO THIS? (Confession, asking for forgiveness from someone, turning away from our sin and toward Jesus.)

Prayer: *God, we know that you have a plan for us, and part of that plan is to fight sin in our lives. Help us turn to you often throughout our day and stay on track with these efforts. We know that we cannot do this alone and need your help. May we stay faithful and true to your work. Amen.*

ZECHARIAH WEEK 30

ZECHARIAH 4-5

Lesson 1 (Zechariah 4:1-14)

Takeaway: Zechariah saw a lampstand continually burning with an unlimited reserve of oil.

Takeaway: This picture represents how only through God will they succeed, not by their own doing and resources.

> **DISCUSSION:** GOD WORKS THROUGH HUMANS TO ACCOMPLISH THINGS. IT IS WITH THE HELP OF HIS STRENGTH, NOT HUMAN STRENGTH, THAT HIS WORK IS DONE. WHAT DO YOU THINK THIS MEANS? (All our gifts are given to us by God; we are nothing without God; God is in control of everything, not us.)

Prayer: *Lord, we are so thankful for all that you have given us and the talents that we have. Help us use them to do your will and never take all that we have for granted. You are a gracious God who gives and loves. We are in awe of you. Amen.*

Lesson 2 (Zechariah 4:1-14)

Takeaway: The responsibility to rebuild the temple in Jerusalem was given to Zerubbabel. (Ezra 3:2,8 and Haggai 1:1)

Takeaway: The prophets Haggai and Zechariah gave the moral and spiritual encouragement while Zerubbabel made sure the task was carried out.

> **DISCUSSION:** ZERUBBABEL DID NOT HAVE TO BE MIGHTY OR POWERFUL TO GET THE JOB DONE. HE ONLY HAD TO

MATERIALS
The Bible

OTHER RESOURCES

Ezra 3:2,8 and Haggai 1:1 for Lesson 2.

Stop, Pray, and Turn the other way from my website for Lesson 4.

NOTE TO TEACHERS
DISCUSSION: WHEN YOU SEE ITEMS IN ALL CAPS, THEY ARE NOTES TO SHARE WITH YOUR CLASS. (Notes in parentheses are notes and thoughts for the teacher.)

WORK THROUGH THE SPIRIT OF GOD. ANYTHING WORTH DOING IS DONE IN THE HANDS OF THE LORD. DO YOU ALLOW GOD TO GUIDE YOU IN YOUR WORK? GIVE AN EXAMPLE OF WHEN GOD DID OR DID NOT GUIDE YOU AND WHAT THAT LOOKED LIKE. (For me, when I pray before I start something and ask God to lead and guide me, I am focused and feel Him working through me. Other times, I am distracted, unsure, or unmotivated, and I can tell it is another spirit wanting me to waste my time and not accomplish the task. I have to stop and remember to pray and refocus myself with God as my strength and guide. The power of prayer!)

Prayer: *Heavenly Father, we pray for your support. Remind us of the importance of prayer before we begin things. Help us allow you to lead everything we do in life by always turning to you first. May we also remember to thank you for all your work throughout our day. Amen.*

Lesson 3 (Zechariah 5:1-4)

Takeaway: The flying scroll that Zechariah sees represents God's curse.

Takeaway: God's Word and Spirit will judge every person.

• •

> **DISCUSSION:** THE CURSE IS GOD'S SYMBOL OF DESTRUCTION WHEN ALL SIN WILL BE JUDGED AND REMOVED. ARE YOU MAKING YOUR LIFE ONE THAT FOLLOWS GOD'S COMMANDS? WE ARE HUMAN AND WILL MAKE MISTAKES, BUT WE HAVE TO GET BACK UP AND KEEP WORKING ON MAKING A CHANGE NEXT TIME WE ARE FACED WITH THE SIN.

Prayer: *God, we have so many temptations in this world that make it very hard to stay focused on our tasks. Help us by continuing to light our way, so we turn to you when we are tempted to do wrong. May we feel your strength and love and change our route. Amen.*

Lesson 4 (Zechariah 5:5-11)

Takeaway: The woman in the basket represents the wickedness of the nations.

Takeaway: She was packed by an angel and sent back to Shinar (Babylon).

> **DISCUSSION:** THE REMOVAL OF SIN IS NECESSARY TO CLEAN UP THE NATION, AND INDIVIDUALS MUST REPENT OF THEIR SINS. DON'T HIDE THEM. WHAT HAPPENS IF WE TRY TO HIDE THEM? (God still knows, our hearts are not cleaned, the sins continue to be within us until we make a change to get them out.)

Prayer: *Lord God, we come to you with any sins we have on our hearts. We give them to you and ask for your help to change our ways. Help us be aware of temptations before we choose to act. May your strength, love, and guidance remind us to stop, pray, and turn the other way. Amen.*

ZECHARIAH WEEK 31

ZECHARIAH 6-7

Lesson 1 (Zechariah 6:1-8)

Takeaway: The four horses and chariots that Zechariah sees represent God's judgment on the world.

Takeaway: The one sent to the north went in the direction from which most of Judah's enemies came from. The other horses stay and patrol the world, waiting on God's command.

> **DISCUSSION:** JUDGMENT COMES IN GOD'S TIMING AND AT HIS COMMAND. WE ARE NOT ALWAYS PUNISHED FOR THINGS RIGHT AWAY. SOMETIMES WE THINK WE GOT AWAY WITH SOMETHING AND THEN THE FEAR OF GETTING CAUGHT EATS AT US AND IS WORSE THAN GETTING CAUGHT RIGHT AWAY. ONE THING NEVER CHANGES, JUDGMENT WILL COME UNLESS WE CONFESS AND MAKE THINGS RIGHT.

Prayer: *Lord, we pray that when we do fail you, as we know we will as humans, that we pick ourselves up and turn to you for forgiveness. Don't allow us to live in a lie or suffer in our hearts with the pain caused by hiding things from you and others. May we acknowledge our mistakes and take action to fix them. Amen.*

MATERIALS

The Bible

NOTES

NOTE TO TEACHERS
DISCUSSION: WHEN YOU SEE ITEMS IN ALL CAPS, THEY ARE NOTES TO SHARE WITH YOUR CLASS. (Notes in parentheses are notes and thoughts for the teacher.)

97

· ·

Lesson 2 (Zechariah 6:9-15)

Takeaway: A king ruled Judah's political life, and the high priest ruled its religious life.

Takeaway: God tells Zechariah that one day someone would be worthy of the crown of both king and priest.

> **DISCUSSION:** GOD HAS GIVEN US CONSISTENT BLESSINGS IN OUR LIVES. WE MUST BE CONSISTENT IN OUR OBEDIENCE WITH HIM AND THANKSGIVING FOR HIS BLESSINGS. LIVE YOUR LIFE TO OBEY AND THANK HIM.

Prayer: *God, we thank you for the commandments and showing us how to live through the example of your Son Jesus. May we live our lives striving to be like your Son and give thanks for all our blessings daily. Amen.*

Lesson 3 (Zechariah 7:1-7)

Takeaway: Zechariah called the Israelites out about their fasting.

Takeaway: They fasted without having the right attitude toward God. They weren't thinking of their sins and why God put them in exile. They were just simply fasting.

> **DISCUSSION:** WE MUST NOT GO THROUGH LIFE DOING THINGS OUT OF HABIT, BUT RATHER DO THEM TO PLEASE GOD AND SHOW HIM WHERE ARE HEARTS ARE. THIS IS NOT JUST ABOUT OUR RELIGIOUS LIFE BUT ALSO OUR SCHOOL WORK, FAMILY TIME, AND REST.

Prayer: *Heavenly Father, we give you our time, hearts, and talents to grow us in whatever way you need us to grow. May each day be one of learning and a promise to continue on our path guided by our faith in you. Help us make the most of everything here on earth. Amen.*

Lesson 4 (Zechariah 7:8-14)

Takeaway: Zechariah reminds the people about how their ancestors received God's wrath when they allowed their hearts to turn away from Him.

Takeaway: He doesn't want them to repeat their ancestor's mistakes and allow this sin to happen again.

> **DISCUSSION:** WE MUST READ GOD'S WORD AND THEN APPLY IT TO OUR LIVES TO PROTECT OURSELVES FROM THE EASY HABIT OF SIN. WE WANT TO SOFTEN OUR HEARTS TO WHAT GOD TEACHES US ABOUT SIN AND CHOOSE HIS WAY.

Prayer: *Thank you, God, for the lessons you provide us in your Word. They are a gift to us. Help us make the most of our time when reading it and help us apply the lessons to our lives. We want to learn each day and better ourselves on our journey with you. Amen.*

ZECHARIAH WEEK 32

ZECHARIAH 8

Lesson 1 (Zechariah 8:1-5)

Takeaway: One day Christ will rule His kingdom here on earth.

Takeaway: In troubled times, the very old and the very young suffer the most, but in this vision, they fill the streets with their normal activities.

> **DISCUSSION:** WE ARE PROMISED PEACE AND PROSPERITY IN GOD'S NEW EARTH. WHEN JESUS RETURNS, HEAVEN AND EARTH WILL BECOME ONE.

Prayer: *Lord, we are in such awe of the returning of your Son Jesus. We pray for the day of unity and peace when your children come together and give you praise. May we be ready for your return, and may you know us as your faithful followers. Amen.*

Lesson 2 (Zechariah 8:6-10)

Takeaway: A small group of God's people returned to Jerusalem to rebuild the temple.

Takeaway: It was a struggle to survive in the land. Others tried to discourage them, but they believed that God would reign in this city and bring peace and prosperity.

> **DISCUSSION:** MATTHEW 19:26 SAYS THAT "WITH GOD ALL THINGS ARE POSSIBLE." OUR GOD CAN DO ANYTHING, EVEN THINGS THAT SEEM UNBELIEVABLE TO YOU AND ME. REMEMBER THIS WHEN YOU ARE FACING WHAT SEEMS LIKE AN IMPOSSIBLE TASK.

MATERIALS
The Bible

OTHER RESOURCES
Matthew 19:26 for Lesson 2.

NOTE TO TEACHERS
DISCUSSION: WHEN YOU SEE ITEMS IN ALL CAPS, THEY ARE NOTES TO SHARE WITH YOUR CLASS. (Notes in parentheses are notes and thoughts for the teacher.)

Prayer: *God, we know that all things are done through you and that you make anything possible. Help us keep that faith in our hearts as we move forward with a task or situation that seems impossible to get through or finish. With you leading the way, we will have faith in doing the work you set forth for us. Amen.*

Lesson 3 (Zechariah 11-17)

Takeaway: God and the prophets had been urging the people to finish building the temple for more than fifteen years. Here, God gives them a vision of the future to encourage them to continue.

Takeaway: We might be tempted to slow down or give up on things when they are too difficult, but God's promise about the future should encourage us to do His work now.

> **DISCUSSION:** GOD KNOWS THE RESULTS OF OUR HARD WORK AND WILL HELP AND GUIDE US AS WE CONTINUE WORKING FOR HIM. LISTEN TO HIS PROMISES AND TRUST IN YOUR FAITH.

Prayer: *Heavenly Father, we thank you for all you do for us. Help us continue to do your work during difficult times. Give us the energy to keep moving forward when we want to stop. May we get the rest we need and your guidance each day to finish our task. Amen.*

Lesson 4 (Zechariah 8:18-23)

Takeaway: The neighboring peoples did not respect the city of Jerusalem because God let enemies punish His people for their sins.

Takeaway: Zechariah says that Jerusalem will be a holy place and highly respected throughout the world because its people will have a change of heart toward God.

• •

DISCUSSION: OTHERS WILL SEE THE GREAT BLESSINGS OF THE LORD AND HOW GOD REWARDS HIS PEOPLE WHO ARE FAITHFUL TO HIM. CONTINUE TO DO HIS WORK AND RECEIVE HIS BLESSINGS AS OTHERS WATCH AND LEARN FROM YOU.

Prayer: *God, we are ready to take on whatever you ask of us. Help us be that light for others who see the blessings you give each day and the way you help and guide us. Remind us to thank you often and be faithful disciples. Amen.*

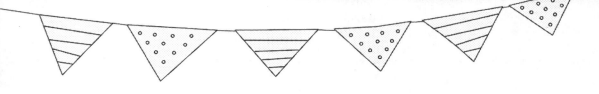

ZECHARIAH WEEK 33

ZECHARIAH 9

Lesson 1 (Zechariah 9:9-10)

Takeaway: The prediction of Jesus riding into Jerusalem is stated here, five hundred years before the event. (Matthew 21:1-11)

Takeaway: Just as Jesus fulfilled the prophecy by coming to the earth, we can be certain the prophecies about His second coming.

> **DISCUSSION:** ARE YOU READY FOR HIS RETURN? HOW DO WE PREPARE FOR THIS? (Have a relationship with Him every day, be prepared for Him to show up and see what we are doing at any time, take time to pray and praise Him daily.)

Prayer: *Lord God, we are so excited for the coming of your Son Jesus. Help us be ready for His return and help others also prepare for His coming. May we be the light for anyone who is in need. Amen.*

Lesson 2 (Zechariah 9:9-10)

Takeaway: In verse nine, he speaks of the first coming of Christ, while verse ten refers to the second coming.

Takeaway: When Christ comes again, He will rule over all nations across the whole earth.

MATERIALS
The Bible

NOTES
Matthew 21:1-11 for Lesson 1.

Philippians 2:9-11 for Lesson 2.

NOTE TO TEACHERS
DISCUSSION: WHEN YOU SEE ITEMS IN ALL CAPS, THEY ARE NOTES TO SHARE WITH YOUR CLASS. (Notes in parentheses are notes and thoughts for the teacher.)

• •

> **DISCUSSION:** PHILIPPIANS 2:9-11 TELLS US THAT "EVERY KNEE WILL BOW TO CHRIST AND EVERY TONGUE WILL CONFESS HIM AS LORD." IMAGINE WHAT THIS WILL LOOK LIKE …

Prayer: *Heavenly Father, we can't even imagine what this day will be like for us when we see you face to face. We just sit and wonder what that might be like and see nothing but beauty and honor for you. We praise you today and always. Amen.*

Lesson 3 (Zechariah 9:11-13)

Takeaway: Just as we would sign our name on a contract today, covenants in the Old Testament were sealed with blood.

Takeaway: Christ would seal the new covenant for His people with the blood He shed at Calvary.

> **DISCUSSION:** JESUS WILL DELIVER US FROM THIS EARTH AND OUR SINS. THROUGH JESUS, WE HAVE BEEN SAVED.

Prayer: *God, we are so thankful for your Son Jesus. Thank you for the example He gave us and the sacrifice He made on the cross. We will forever be grateful and follow the path that He has given us. Amen.*

Lesson 4 (Zechariah 9:14-17)

Takeaway: The kingdom was divided after Solomon's reign into the northern kingdom (Israel or Ephraim) and the southern kingdom (Judah with Jerusalem as the capital).

Takeaway: This prophecy says that all of Israel, north and south, will be reunited.

> **DISCUSSION:** GOD CAN HELP US OVERCOME WAR AND OUR SINS. ASK FOR GOD'S HELP. HE IS ALWAYS THERE.

Prayer: *At times, we think we can never work things out with a friend who has upset us or with a sibling that annoys us, but when we turn to you, Lord, we know that your power is better than anything. Help us come to you with our sins instead of fighting with others. We need you in our lives daily. Amen.*

ZECHARIAH WEEK 34

ZECHARIAH 10

Lesson 1 (Zechariah 10:1-4)

Takeaway: Zechariah preached more than five hundred years before Christ came, yet he described Him to a T.

Takeaway: He called him the "cornerstone," the "tent peg," the "battle bow," and a "ruler."

> **DISCUSSION:** ZECHARIAH DESCRIBES JESUS AS STRONG, STABLE, TRUSTWORTHY, AND A MAN OF ACTION. WHAT A PERFECT EXAMPLE JESUS IS! JESUS FULFILLS ALL OF THE PROMISES TO GOD'S PEOPLE.

Prayer: *God, we thank you for your Son Jesus and the wonderful example He is for us. No one could ever be as strong as Him or do what He did on the cross. We know that His love for us is eternal. We can trust Him for direction and guidance in life. Help us allow Him to be active in our lives and walk alongside us each day as we remember to pray and ask for His presence. Amen.*

Lesson 2 (Zechariah 10:5-6)

Takeaway: Judah represents the southern kingdom, and Israel represents the northern kingdom.

Takeaway: God plans to bring all of His people together.

> **DISCUSSION:** THE PEOPLE IN THE NORTHERN KINGDOM WERE LIVING THEIR LIVES IN A VERY WORLDLY WAY. WHAT DOES THIS MEAN? (Not putting God first, doing what everyone else is doing even if it's wrong, loving themselves before others.) ONLY GOD COULD ACCOMPLISH BRINGING ALL THESE PEOPLE TOGETHER.

MATERIALS

The Bible

NOTES

NOTE TO TEACHERS
DISCUSSION: WHEN YOU SEE ITEMS IN ALL CAPS, THEY ARE NOTES TO SHARE WITH YOUR CLASS. (Notes in parentheses are notes and thoughts for the teacher.)

Prayer: *Lord, we know that you want to bring everyone close to you. Not only do we want to draw close to you ourselves, but we want to help others also know who you are. Only you have the power to open people's hearts, so they are willing to hear what you have to say. May we do our part in your work here on earth to bring everyone as one nation under God. Amen.*

Lesson 3 (Zechariah 10:7-12)

Takeaway: When we allow ourselves to stay close to God, He will help us through the obstacles in life.

Takeaway: When we choose to move away from God, other influences distract our decision-making, and we can forget to ask for God's help.

> **DISCUSSION:** GOD PROMISES TO MAKE US STRONG IN ANY TASK THAT HE GIVES US IN LIFE! DOES BEING STRONG MEAN BEING SUCCESSFUL? (No, it could mean doing what is right, learning from a mistake, being able to admit we are wrong.)

Prayer: *Heavenly Father, we know that the only strength that matters in life is the strength that comes from you. When we allow ourselves to feel good about something that draws us away from you, we are feeding off of human strength, and that never compares to you. May we always take the time to tap into your power before beginning anything. Amen.*

Lesson 4 (Zechariah 10:7-12)

Takeaway: The "sea of affliction" in verse eleven refers to the Red Sea.

Takeaway: God delivered the Israelites from slavery in Egypt by having them cross this sea.

> **DISCUSSION:** GOD WOULD PROTECT THE ISRAELITES AGAIN AS THEY RETURNED FROM EGYPT AND OTHER LANDS. GOD ALWAYS PROTECTS US AND NEVER GIVES UP ON US.

Prayer: *God, we think of all the miracles from the stories we have read in the Bible and see your power. Help us see that in the little things in our lives each day. May we stop to count our blessings and see how you work miracles regularly. Amen.*

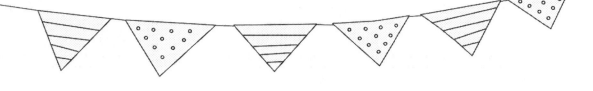

ZECHARIAH WEEK 35

ZECHARIAH 11

Lesson 1 (Zechariah 11:1-17)

Takeaway: God told Zechariah to act as two different shepherds.

Takeaway: One demonstrated how God would reject His people when they rejected Him (verses 4-14), and the other how God would let His people fall into the hands of evil shepherds (verses 15-17).

> **DISCUSSION:** ONLY JESUS CAN SHEPHERD GOD'S PEOPLE. WHENEVER YOU ARE UNSURE OF SOMETHING, JESUS IS THE ONE TO TURN TO FOR GUIDANCE IN THIS WORLD.

Prayer: *Lord, help us always turn to Jesus. We know there will be times that will be hard for us to do this. Help our hearts feel your love and give us the strength to push the sin away. We need your light in our lives. Amen.*

Lesson 2 (Zechariah 11:7-12)

Takeaway: Zechariah took two shepherd's staffs and named them Beauty, meaning Grace, and Bonds, meaning Union.

Takeaway: He broke the first one to show how God's covenant with His people was broken, and the second one to show that the brotherhood between Judah and Israel was also broken.

MATERIALS

The Bible

Stop, Pray, and Turn the Other Way for Lesson 2.

OTHER RESOURCES

Matthew 27:3-5 for Lesson 3.

NOTE TO TEACHERS
DISCUSSION: WHEN YOU SEE ITEMS IN ALL CAPS, THEY ARE NOTES TO SHARE WITH YOUR CLASS. (Notes in parentheses are notes and thoughts for the teacher.)

> **DISCUSSION:** THE SHEEP REPRESENTED THE PEOPLE HUNGRY WITH GREED AND SIN. THIS CHAPTER ALSO SHOWS US THAT PEOPLE DON'T GET AWAY WITH THIS FOREVER, AS GOD DOES JUDGE THEM. WHAT SHOULD WE DO WHEN WE ARE FEELING GREEDY OR HAVING SINFUL THOUGHTS? (Pray, ask for God's help, start doing the opposite thing than what you are doing. Hang Stop, Pray, and Turn the Other Way in the classroom as a reminder.)

Prayer: *Lord God, we know that we mess up as humans and sin. Help us confess our sins and repent. Give us the strength we need to stop sinning and make a better choice. May we remember to Stop, Pray, and Turn the Other Way when tempted. Amen.*

Lesson 3 (Zechariah 11:12-13)

Takeaway: It was an insult to pay the shepherd thirty pieces of silver because this is what someone would pay for a slave.

Takeaway: This was the same amount that Judas was paid for betraying Jesus.

> **DISCUSSION:** THE PRICE FOR JESUS WAS THE SAME AS A SLAVE! READ MATTHEW 27:3-5 AND SEE JUDAS'S REGRET. WHAT CAN WE DO WHEN WE HAVE REGRETS ABOUT SOMETHING? (Pray, say you are sorry, talk to an adult, go to confession.)

Prayer: *Heavenly Father, help us do the right thing when we have made a mistake or done something wrong. Give us the strength to admit when we are wrong and the courage to say we are sorry. May we turn to you and other Christians to help us through the trial. Amen.*

Lesson 4 (Zechariah 111:15-17)

Takeaway: Israel would reject the true shepherd and accept a foolish one instead.

Takeaway: The foolish shepherd would serve his own needs rather than His flock and would destroy them rather than protect them.

> **DISCUSSION:** GOD IS DISPLEASED WHEN PEOPLE ARE NOT FOLLOWING THEIR LEADERS AND WHEN A LEADER DOES NOT DO HIS JOB. HOW CAN WE HELP THE LEADERS IN OUR LIVES? (Listen to them, don't give them attitude, and be a good example to others.) HOW CAN WE BE GOOD LEADERS IN OUR LIVES? (Get along with our siblings, take charge of what needs to be done when Mom and Dad are gone, be a good example for others at school or on the ball field.)

Prayer: *God, we want to be good leaders in our community, school, and home. Help us put others before ourselves by loving them as we would want to be loved. We pray for the leaders in our lives. May we be respectful and kind to them in our actions and attitudes. Amen.*

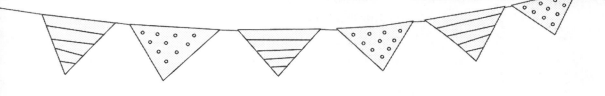

ZECHARIAH WEEK 36

ZECHARIAH 12-13

Lesson 1 (Zechariah 12:1-9)

Takeaway: The countryside of Judah (the tents) would have priority over the city of Jerusalem so that the people of Jerusalem would not become too **proud**.

- ◆ *Pride (proud)* – a feeling of deep pleasure or satisfaction from one's own achievements.

Takeaway: Christ came to seek and save all, not just the rich, famous, and well-known.

> **DISCUSSION:** DON'T ALLOW PRIDE TO GET IN YOUR WAY OF KNOWING WHO JESUS IS. GIVE IT TO GOD!

Prayer: *Lord, help us not be prideful in our lives. When good things happen, help us see your work in it all and give the glory to you. We know that nothing is accomplished without you. May we be content in doing your work in your name. Amen.*

Lesson 2 (Zechariah 12:10-14)

Takeaway: Fifty days after Christ's resurrection, the Holy Spirit was poured out at Pentecost. (Acts 2:1-4)

Takeaway: It is the Spirit that reveals God to us and that helps us through our weaknesses and sin.

> **DISCUSSION:** ONE DAY ALL THE PEOPLE WILL KNOW JESUS AND HIS CRUCIFIXION WILL BRING GREAT

MATERIALS
The Bible

OTHER RESOURCES
Acts 2:1-4 for Lesson 2.

John 4:13-14 for Lesson 3.

NOTE TO TEACHERS
DISCUSSION: WHEN YOU SEE ITEMS IN ALL CAPS, THEY ARE NOTES TO SHARE WITH YOUR CLASS. (Notes in parentheses are notes and thoughts for the teacher.)

• •

MOURNING. THERE WILL BE AN AWAKENING OF SORROW FOR SIN. HOW CAN YOU CALL ON THE HOLY SPIRIT TO HELP YOU WITH SIN? (Pray and ask, confess when you sin and ask for help to change, pray daily to ask for a shield to fight against a daily sin you encounter.)

Prayer: *Lord God, we feel the Holy Spirit working in our hearts and are so thankful to be blessed with a relationship with you. Help us reach out and grasp the Spirit for help and guidance in our day. May you guide us, give us the words we need to say, and have the love in our hearts to do your work. Amen.*

Lesson 3 (Zechariah 13:1-6)

Takeaway: A fountain represents the never-ending supply of God's forgiveness.

Takeaway: In John 4:13-14, Jesus talks of His "living water" that brings everlasting life.

DISCUSSION: THE LIVING WORD, JESUS, AND THE WRITTEN WORD, THE BIBLE, WILL SATISFY YOU COMPLETELY WHEN YOUR HEART IS OPEN. WHAT DO YOU THINK THIS MEANS? (Jesus was living proof of how to live, when you learn things from the Bible on how to live you understand God's plan, we have both the Bible and Jesus to draw us closer to God, the only way to Heaven is through Jesus.)

Prayer: *Heavenly Father, we know that the only way to Heaven is through your Son Jesus. Help us grow in our relationship with Him and drink from the fountain of your forgiveness. May we turn our focus on you, God, and look forward to celebrating your glory with you one day in Heaven. Amen.*

Lesson 4 (Zechariah 13:7-9)

Takeaway: "One-third" is a small part of the world.

Takeaway: God said that a righteous remnant still trusted and followed Him.

DISCUSSION: ARE YOU IN THAT SMALL PART OF THE WORLD THAT IS OBEDIENT TO GOD? OBEY GOD NO MATTER WHAT, EVEN THROUGH TRIALS AND HARD TIMES AND YOU WILL BE PURIFIED AND MADE MORE LIKE JESUS.

Prayer: *God, we are so committed to following your ways through all the good and bad that can come in life. Help us stay faithful, and remind us of your directions for us in the Ten Commandments. May we always think of how your Son Jesus would do things and follow in His footsteps. Amen.*

ZECHARIAH WEEK 37

ZECHARIAH 14

Lesson 1 (Zechariah 14:1-15)

Focusing on verse four.

Takeaway: Jesus spoke with His disciples on the Mount of Olives. (Matthew 24)

Takeaway: An angel appeared near this mountain and promised that Jesus would return the same way He left. (Acts 1:11)

> **DISCUSSION:** JESUS TELLS HIS DISCIPLES ABOUT THE FUTURE, HIS RETURN, AND TO REMAIN WATCHFUL ON THE MOUNT OF OLIVES. THE ANGEL REMINDS US THAT HE WILL RETURN. BE READY FOR HIM BY STUDYING SCRIPTURE CAREFULLY AND LIVING THE WAY HE INTENDED FOR YOU.

Prayer: *Lord, we are encouraged to watch for the day of your Son's return. Help us prepare by making good choices in how we spend our time here on earth. Allow us to see your teachings through your Word and the example of your Son. May we grow closer to you in the process and find peace and contentment in life. Amen.*

Lesson 2 (Zechariah 14:1-15)

Focusing on verse five.

Takeaway: God knows who His people are.

Takeaway: God will protect those who turn to Him in life.

MATERIALS
The Bible

OTHER RESOURCES
Matthew 24 and Acts 1:11 for Lesson 1.

NOTE TO TEACHERS
DISCUSSION: WHEN YOU SEE ITEMS IN ALL CAPS, THEY ARE NOTES TO SHARE WITH YOUR CLASS. (Notes in parentheses are notes and thoughts for the teacher.)

113

• •

> **DISCUSSION:** JESUS SAID THAT BEFORE HE RETURNS, THE MESSAGE OF SALVATION WOULD BE PREACHED THROUGHOUT THE WORLD. THIS WAS THE MISSION OF THE DISCIPLES AND IS STILL OUR MISSION TODAY. ARE YOU BEING A DISCIPLE OF CHRIST? (Share how God works in your life with others, praying for others, praying with others.)

Prayer: *Lord God, we are so thankful for all that you are and all that we have. Help us be the disciples that you need us to be and give us the correct words and the right direction to go in life. Help us show others your love through our hearts and help them to turn to you in their lives each day. Amen.*

Lesson 3 (Zechariah 14:16-21)

Takeaway: God will fulfill the dreams of the people of Jerusalem beyond their imagination.

Takeaway: He wants to do the same for us today.

> **DISCUSSION:** THE STEPS WE TAKE EACH DAY WITH THE LORD BY OUR SIDE WILL OPEN OUR HEARTS TO DISCOVER MORE OF HOW GOD WORKS DAY BY DAY. ALLOW ALL THINGS IN YOUR LIFE TO WORK THROUGH THE LORD.

Prayer: *Heavenly Father, help us stop and pray before we begin things each day. Allow us to bring you into all that we do, think, and say throughout our lives. When we let you lead, we allow you to be in charge of our lives and can see the work you do each day. May we see you in it all. Amen.*

Lesson 4 (Zechariah 14:16-21)

Takeaway: Zechariah spoke to people who were going through hard times.

Takeaway: God promised to restore their land, city, and temple.

> **DISCUSSION:** THROUGH ZECHARIAH'S MESSAGE, WE LEARN THAT OUR HOPE IS ALWAYS FOUND IN GOD. GOD, AND ONLY GOD, IS IN CONTROL OF THE WORLD!

Prayer: *God, we pray for our families, our school, our community, and our world. We trust it all to you. Help us grow, love, and see your work as we continue to read, learn about you, and share your love with others. Amen.*

ABOUT THE AUTHOR

Cheryl is a Pre-K teacher at Saint Bonaventure in Columbus, NE. She has been devoted to reading and studying the Bible since 2014 and has a passion for sharing it with children, teachers and parents.

Her experience with children has taught her that being a kid at heart is what allows others to open up and trust in you. Showing others how God came into her life and completely changed it is something she wants to share with the youth, teachers and parents of our Catholic Schools.

Before starting her job at Saint Bonaventure School, she did some substituting in other parochial schools when needed, and one thing that they all had in common no matter which school she taught at or which grade she was in, that they all began their day with time in God's Word.

Being hired as a Pre-K teacher, she started her mission in her first year with her students and made the Bible her top priority each day and used the lessons to grow and connect as a class. The results were amazing! Parents were wanting to know what she was doing and was excited about their child wanting to read the Bible together at home.

Ever since she began teaching, she has been especially drawn to helping children, teachers and parents to connect through their faith with a love for Jesus. God has given her a gift to help others make a difference in the world in their own amazing way, by allowing God to lead them.

Cheryl was one of the second group of Catholics who went through the Mentorship Program for training through the Omaha Diocese. She taught her first work shop on How to Teach the Bible zoom style during the spring of 2020.

With her teaching of children for 30+ years of students from preschool through the 8th grade, she has developed years of experience. She has been a Childcare Provider, a Classroom Teacher and a Wednesday night PRE Program Instructor.

Cheryl is on a God driven mission to encourage others to put God at the top of their day and to be dedicated to see it through.

She feels that in order to help prepare our kids for life outside of Catholic School, we have to give them something more than a safe space at school or at home. We have to give them the Bible. We do this by going through it with them day by day and school year by school year.

Pre-K	**Children Bible Stories from Genesis through Ruth**
Kindergarten	**Covers the entire book of 1 Samuel**
First Grade	**Covers both Esther and Job**
Second Grade	**Covers the entire book of Jeremiah**
Third Grade	**Begins in Jonah and goes through Zechariah**
Fourth Grade	**Covers the entire book of Mark**
Fifth Grade	**Covers both Ephesians and Philippians**
Sixth Grade	**Covers both Philemon and Hebrews**

**For additional downloadable resources,
visit www.InSchoolWithJesus.com**

**If you would like to arrange for
a speaker or additional training (in person or online),
visit www.InSchoolWithJesus.com**

Made in the USA
Columbia, SC
05 October 2023

23988912R00074